Global Lean

Seeing the New Waste Rooted in Communication, Distance, and Culture

Global Lean

Seeing the New Waste Rooted in Communication, Distance, and Culture

Samuel Yankelevitch

CRC Press
Taylor & Francis Group
Boca Raton London New York

CRC Press is an imprint of the
Taylor & Francis Group, an **informa** business

A PRODUCTIVITY PRESS BOOK

CRC Press
Taylor & Francis Group
6000 Broken Sound Parkway NW, Suite 300
Boca Raton, FL 33487-2742

Printed on acid-free paper
Version Date: 20160818

International Standard Book Number-13: 978-1-4987-7334-8 (Paperback)

Library of Congress Cataloging-in-Publication Data

Names: Yankelevitch, Sam, author.
Title: Global lean : seeing the new waste rooted in communication, distance, and culture / Samuel Yankelevitch.
Description: Boca Raton, FL : CRC Press, 2016. | Includes bibliographical references and index.
Identifiers: LCCN 2016023252 | ISBN 9781498773348 (alk. paper)
Subjects: LCSH: International business enterprises--Managementt. | Management--Cross-cultural studies. | Organizational effectiveness--Cross-cultural studies. | Production control.
Classification: LCC HD62.4 .Y355 2016 | DDC 658.4/013--dc23
LC record available at https://lccn.loc.gov/2016023252

Visit the Taylor & Francis Web site at
http://www.taylorandfrancis.com

and the CRC Press Web site at
http://www.crcpress.com

This book is dedicated to Aron Levy, my grandfather and my mentor, who insisted that the most valuable assets in our business are the human beings that individually contribute to getting things done collectively. Regardless of the global developments and technological advances he would never see, and the ones I will never see, I believe humans will still have to interact with each other to accomplish those things that cannot be done independently.

Whether we interact effectively or not, is our choice.

Contents

Foreword

Sam Yankelevitch provides us with a moving and all too recognizable story of a successful business driven to the brink of disaster by the upper management's failure to recognize the emerging business process constraints. Building on Lean and his understanding of the theory of constraints, Yankelevitch points out barriers and bottlenecks are not necessarily only within the four walls of our plants. In fact, some of our most vexing limitations may not be directly related to a physical transformation process at all.

Today, the complexity inherent in our global supply chains and the myriad of ways they intersect and interact with our operational processes create unique challenges that we are only now beginning to understand. From a Lean perspective, unidirectional messaging enabled through electronic channels such as email, information extracted from less than perfect software platforms, and language differences that exist among employees from different parts of the world who must work together can all create waste. Within the global enterprise, the gemba extends beyond the four walls of our service facilities or manufacturing plants, and into our supply chains.

Language, distance, and cultural differences contribute to variance—that in turn helps generate waste and this work traces specific examples that are typical to our global supply chains and our facilities. Yankelevitch points out that clear, unambiguous communication is required to reduce these variances. Thus, the road to supply chain waste elimination must include the detection, naming, and measuring of the variances caused by miscommunication.

The good news that Yankelevitch suggests is that new tools are not required to solve these emerging issues. Instead, the process improvement tools and the perspectives of Lean and Six Sigma, when used creatively and with determination can help us deal with the most frustrating communication and cultural issues inherent in working together across large distances. Process improvement experts, schooled in Lean and Six Sigma will recognize the tools of 5S, the PDCA cycle, VSM, and root cause analysis. However, they may not be familiar with the ways Yankelevitch demonstrates how these tools can be adapted to recognize where the value is being added, reduce variation, and eliminate waste in the supply chain communication processes that connect our operations.

This work presents us with a modern day parable. But instead of concluding with a moral, Yankelevitch provides a systematic process, integrated with well-understood tools, that will help any manager struggling to identify and eliminate waste-creating complexity and ambiguity that infects all our global supply chains.

Dr. John B. Jensen
Managing Director of the Global Supply Chain and Process Management Center
Darla Moore School of Business
University of South Carolina

Preface

When our world was hit by the Industrial Revolution which started in the eighteenth century, a wave of individuals and companies were motivated to come up with faster and cheaper ways to mass produce goods in order to satisfy an ambitious population moving from farming to urban living.

Most of these production systems focused on discrete, localized solutions where expansions of manufacturing facilities were often achieved within the same country and by using cookie-cutter formulas that had proven to be effective. Growth was made possible in the circumstances that these organizations were operating in.

Globalization is a newer wave that has been hitting our economies and it has changed the business context we once knew and were comfortable with. What worked once, might not be working so well today.

The need to integrate people and companies from different countries is continually shifting the way we were used to interacting and transacting in the direction of the goals and objectives of our organizations.

Manufacturing processes were once physically contained within the four walls, and we could walk around and directly observe as things were happening. With today's degree of globalization, many of those processes have been dispersed over thousands of miles, across oceans and different time zones.

We can no longer go see every process and are critically dependent on the effective coordination of actions between players in different countries and continents. To get the right things done, teams of people are interacting virtually, either by email, phone, or through videoconferencing. They continually transmit their ideas and requests via engineering drawings and specifications, IT systems, and through operating instructions.

It surely seems like today the amount of interactions and communication required to get results is much greater, and certainly more complex.

The gemba[1] that we once knew has changed dramatically. In order to see the whole—and grasp the issues confronted by organizations today—we have to become aware of the obstacles that are part and parcel of globalization. However, we seem to be too busy to acknowledge these obstacles, and bring them to the surface and deal with them.

Going to the gemba and witnessing the territory with our own eyes allows us to see objectively as things are happening, it's the only way to directly observe and see the "what is" versus "what should be," absent of biased interpretations by others or by stale data and personal opinions.

The Polish-American scientist and philosopher Alfred Korzybski articulated the concept of: "the map is not the territory"[2] and in business, going to the gemba is the most direct way to check the map against the territory. When we are unable to directly make this check, then it's possible that over time we begin to confuse, as Korzybski states, "our models of reality with what is really happening." What is real gets clouded in our minds by what should be.

While it's not easy to accept that a wide gap exists between our map and the real world we are acting in, we can sense something is not quite right, things are not working like they used to and then our balance sheet confirms that our map is incorrect—and our customers find somewhere else to buy.

Circumstances and Toyota

In the 1950s when Toyota started their journey to rebuild and grow a company that has very effectively demonstrated how continuous improvement concepts work, they were able to maintain their focus on factory floor issues and the value being added by every step in their own assembly process and in their suppliers' processes. A main reason for this is that Japanese was the language everyone spoke, players shared a national culture, and most of the suppliers were within hours of Toyota's assembly plants. These factors made it easy to effectively exchange close to perfect signals between the customer and the suppliers.

To clarify any doubt about a detail on an order, an instruction or a drawing—a quick personal meeting or hallway conversation would take care of most issues. If something did not go according to plan, every player was within relatively close proximity to react quickly and determine what happened and how to correct it.

Cause and effect were close in time and distance, which helped identify and correlate the sources of problems.

In this sense, the circumstances in which Toyota was operating were local which made it quite advantageous to dedicate most improvement efforts to the process of material transformation and establish the foundation of a very robust and successful production system.

As outside observers, it is easy to miss the invisible factor that effective communication played in the development of their world-famous production and management system.

Today, those same factors have become more critical to the success of any international enterprise and if not attended to, can become barriers that introduce new risks and threats.

Fast Forward to the Twenty-First Century

For many corporations, local is no longer a reality: global is inescapably the new reality. The map they are living by no longer reflects the territory.

Today, to get things done globally, there are substantially more steps than there were in a local world. Many of these additional steps require closer coordination, cooperation, and collaboration between the stakeholders—all of which require clear, direct, and unambiguous communication.

In addition, customer expectations cannot be predicted based on the past and their tastes seem to be changing faster than before. This fact requires a higher degree of focus and alignment for teams that are spread across continents and time zones, trying to coordinate activities effectively in a predominantly virtual environment.

TWENTY-FIRST CENTURY INTERACTIONS

When your enterprise is located within four walls, it is possible to walk the gemba and directly observe the activities that are taking place within your many processes. With globalization, this may be a little more challenging. For one, the physical distance makes it more difficult to visit every process and directly observe what is happening. We rely more on the accuracy of the data and interpretations to understand how efficient and effective our processes might be. Our inability to grasp the situation directly as it is happening is exacerbated because the greater physical distance tends to drive a longer time between cause and

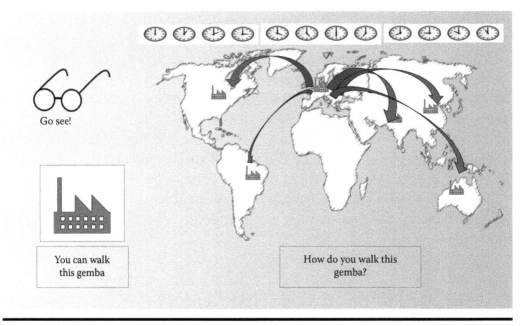

Figure P.1 For many companies the new gemba is no longer inside four walls.

effect. This means that by the time we have figured out what is going on, it may be too late or problems have just gotten bigger. The new gemba requires a lot more coordinated interactions between people from different countries, which means we must implement a way where we communicate effectively and the information and knowledge we need to convey is clearly understood by every player in this new industrial setting. With globalization it is more about the quality of our interactions that will make us or break us. The good thing is that it is possible to adopt Lean thinking to improve this, by applying our continuous improvement knowledge to the process of communication (Figure P.1).

The "Soft" Issues?

Honestly, just labeling a problem "soft" does not make it go away, and it's possible some of us have witnessed the very "hard" cost impact that these so-called "soft issues" have on quality and delivery.

Organizations that use the pretext or get distracted by labeling communication problems "soft issues" will not deal with these with the same level of urgency as other issues.

Countless CEOs prefer to delegate the "soft" to their human resources teams who they see as responsible for taking care of such matters. Others may combine this approach with the acquisition of the latest technology that promises to solve the problems encountered by virtual collaboration and the coordination of activities of different players on an international stage.

However, this is not a task for one specific functional area nor can technology solve every problem or situation.

HR alone cannot be successful in fixing operational or coordination procedures that were designed to function in a specific, local environment that is no longer the same. Similarly, technology can only help solve the limited scope of issues to which its algorithms and programs were originally set up and typically gets confused when circumstances change and unforeseen situations occur.

Cross-Functionality and the Quickening of Interdependence

There is more and more discussion in business books, journals, and the social media on the topic of moving away from verticality in the direction of clearly defined horizontal organizations.

Revisiting the analogy of the map and the territory, the traditional organizational chart depicts a map by which people supposedly interact in closely defined vertical functions and reporting structures, without an explicit design to guide the horizontal interactions required between different functional areas to produce value.

Globalization, in a sense, is serving us a quickening to drive the redesign that clearly defines, for example, who needs to interact with whom, and when—cross-functionally to create the required value for the customer.

One main reason is that globalization exposes the brutal reality of interdependence as a key dynamic required to drive effective execution—and help keep the customer satisfied. While each company is free to act independently, this perceived independence is only an illusion. Like it or not, the reality is that with globalization more and more of our organizations have become inescapably interdependent with other organizations.

As a first step, acknowledging that interdependence exists might require an effort to redefine the existing roles and responsibilities. Then, perhaps creating new roles that ensure cross-functionality, so that effective decisions can be made that consider influences across the whole enterprise.

In a nutshell, interdependence creates a different meaning for the hats each of us wear in business.

This could be a challenge in organizations where employees may wear just one hat that represents a single function. Those employees will have to accept a new definition of their role, where in some instances they will have to wear multiple hats. Going against the current and negating these new responsibilities could sustain the deep-rooted habit of driving decisions to solve matters for one individual player or function, which might actually exacerbate problems for other interdependent players.

People Have to Connect

In their *Harvard Business Review* article "Decoding the DNA of the Toyota Production System,"[3] Steven Spear and H. Kent Brown summarize and dissect some key building blocks of a management system that has become a most important benchmark for many companies. While the article emphasizes the fact that the scientific method is in fact what keeps the system ticking, the authors of the article also list some basic rules that are followed, namely: how people work, how people connect, how the production line is constructed, and how to improve.

"How people connect" is a prerequisite for any endeavor that requires more than one person to perform a specific task. It is evidently tied to the interdependence that exists between every individual player who has some influence in a supply chain of a product or a service—and it presupposes this for interdependence to function effectively and efficiently. Therefore, a rule must exist to prevent any lack of clarity or ambiguity that can create a misunderstanding.

The coordination of every activity is preceded by some type of idea, request, offer, expectation, or decision. Therefore, the degree of clarity conveyed through any of these forms will have an impact on how the activity is executed. In a global context, how people connect is perhaps the most important rule, yet one that most often we pay the least amount of attention because it's easier to notice and maintain focus on the physical: the movement of things, the transformation of materials into components, or the assembly of components into a finished product.

As many of us have not truly followed the suggested rule of Toyota about creating a standardized way in which every connection should happen between two or more people, there is substantial waste created in both the physical, material realm and the less visible dimension of communication. Perhaps, some organizations pay lip service to the topic, but in too many cases, the notorious theme of miscommunication, turf wars, and silos is still only a discussion with little or no solutions.

To make matters more interesting, the fact that we are now not only interdependent in a local sense, but also in a global sense has magnified this previously hidden factor as projects get delayed, things don't get done, or they get done incorrectly.

It's possible that in the past we could assume that what we were saying in plain English to our local employees would be understood with 100% clarity. That was a flawed assumption then and undoubtedly we should avoid assuming the same today, considering we have supply chain partners that may speak our language with less fluency, have different understandings of the words because of their cultural nuances, added to the impact physical distances might have on the degree of clarity.

The magnification of the problem has created serious opportunities for additional costs and non-value-added activities, which are now exposed and more visible.

Our training in the continuous improvement philosophy consistently teaches us to determine a north that is tied to satisfying the expectations of a customer. This is what pushes us to look out for value in every activity associated with this north and devise methodologies and processes to uncover non-value-added waste, and ways to reduce or remove it.

When we realize that the process of communication can also be improved with similar methodologies as the ones we use on production-related processes, it's possible we will uncover waste we had not seen before and that can help the organization remain competitive, grow, and thrive.

The Lean Advantage

Lean as a way of thinking has reached critical mass in the arena of continuous improvement methodologies. In the past 40 years, it has been introduced into the health care, finance, and retail sectors and of course widely used in manufacturing environments.

Nonetheless, each of these sectors is currently being subjected to new forces of globalization that might not have been considered when an organization was originally conceived.

When the word Lean was originally coined,[4] it was tied to the word manufacturing and most of the work done started out in companies dedicated to the transformation of materials into finished tangible goods. The use of Lean, therefore, might be limited to specific traditional areas where value is being transformed in the physical sense, such as a production environment where materials follow a process of transformation until a finished good is produced and delivered to a customer.

Other processes that were not seen as directly affecting the physical transformation processes may have been overlooked and relegated to a lower priority—or as mentioned before, labeled as soft issues for a specific department to deal with.

As the context of our organizations has shifted, Lean thinking cannot remain fixed and unchanged. Instead, we should complement its use on processes that we did not see as important in the past, but that today we cannot hide from. You may consider some ideas in this book as a next generation for Lean, or the "continuous improvement" of a remarkable continuous improvement methodology.

If, for example, the effective coordination of activities in an interdependent world requires accurate and clear communication, we could certainly apply our Lean thinking ways and methodology to ensure that every interaction between two or more individuals required to accomplish a task is adding value.

This means that ideas and instructions should flow with as few obstacles as possible.

Surely, we could consider not changing our Lean focus and keep it limited to local use. However, it's quite possible that our local decisions may create a negative impact on interrelated processes in another organization—and this goes against the idea of seeing and considering the whole picture before a process is defined and standardized.

Globalization means we have people from different countries who speak different languages and are shaped by different cultures. English as the lingua franca[5] of business has not proven to be a successful formula, and I believe that Lean can complement the solutions needed to reduce waste in the interactions of supply chain players.

We are living in the age of the new gemba where our old ways of using Lean may not be as effective as they could be. This is our fork in the road where we could decide to keep our head in the sand or embrace the situation and approach it with the help of some incredible methodologies we already know.

Lean has its own clearly defined language, a process-based approach and a firm dependence on the interaction of people from every level and from every area of the company to continuously improve every aspect of a company.

In this new gemba, the very same people we have trained and involved in improving our processes and solving problems can play a big part in reducing the waste generated by globalization.

Some of the inherent advantages that Lean has are associated with the culture it can create, the clarity in the concepts, and the language it uses. Lean thinking has proven to be a robust way to lead and manage organizations, and companies that have embraced its management system have proven they can remain competitive.

There is yet another very important Lean thinking lesson that needs to be promoted and implemented: Lean points out the need to take care of even the smallest problems and remove or diminish them while they are small. If we allow these to grow, perhaps the solutions will take longer and might be too taxing for us and our teams to solve.

Every industry is now under tremendous competitive pressures with players from countries we never had to worry about entering our markets. When every detail, every second, and every obstacle makes a difference in our survival and growth it's imperative we start to uncover the "small" problems that are hidden from plain sight and take advantage of our problem solving methodologies to find adequate solutions.

This book is intended to expose some of the pitfalls and challenges and offers some ideas on approaching and solving them, using Lean thinking.

Sam Yankelevitch
South Carolina

Author

Samuel Yankelevitch is an author, trainer, and speaker, whose expertise is focused on the problems organizations are experiencing dealing with the increasing complexity of supply chains in the twenty-first century. In his most recent corporate role, as a former vice president and general manager of a German automotive supplier, Sam was responsible for the company's US and Mexico operations.

For more than 30 years, Sam has managed operations in international environments where execution depended highly on effective communication for things to get done on time and within budget.

He is currently the CEO of Xpress Lingo Solutions, a leader in communication improvement processes and intercultural programs, specializing in the automotive and manufacturing sectors' growing need for clear focus, aligned teams and fast response.

Sam has designed several training programs such as *Bridging Cultures to Drive Performance, Lean Communication, A3 Effective Problem Solving System*, and several technical language programs.

He has presented at conferences, symposiums, and professional group events such as the American Society for Quality, South Carolina MEP Lean Alliance, Automation Alley in Detroit, Michigan, University of South Carolina Darla Moore School of Business and Syracuse Supply Chain Improvement Symposium, and most recently in Mexico at the international ADERIAC congress and the Tecnológico de Monterrey, in San Luis Potosi.

He has trained personnel from companies such as BMW, Lear, Novem, Stueken, JCI, and several others that have global operations.

In order to get his message out about the use of Lean to improve the process of communication, Sam coauthored *Lean Potion #9: Communication: The Next Lean Frontier* and *Lean Communication: Applications for Continuous Process Improvement*, where he combines his Lean journey and global and operational experience toward solutions for reducing the waste rooted in misunderstandings, a topic which is further developed in his book *Global Lean: Seeing the Waste Rooted in Communication, Distance and Culture.*

Sam earned a BSc in industrial engineering and an executive masters in financial management. He is fully bilingual Spanish-English and is well versed in German, French, and Italian.

Introduction

Throughout my career I was exposed to work with people from other countries. I traveled to purchase tools and equipment in Spain, Italy, Germany, and China and materials and components from Malaysia, the Philippines, and Poland. I also established new markets in Mexico, Central America, and the Caribbean.

My interactions with people in those countries were through a combination of fax, emails, and personal visits and at all times, I was exposed to the world of misunderstandings and miscommunication, many times leading to frustration, aggravation, and costs.

As I reflected on the fact that communication is a process and that Lean can be extremely effective to improve processes, I coauthored an initial book on the subject with Clair F. Kuhl: *Lean Potion #9: Communication: The Next Lean Frontier*[6] where we shared some concepts and ways of applying Toyota's philosophies to solve communication problems.

Since that book was published I have trained and consulted with large, medium, and small companies that are going through the pains of globalization where cultural differences, a lack of a common language, and physical distance are impacting their projects and ongoing operations.

One common thread many of these companies shared was their understanding of Lean concepts and methodologies and most have been trained and have experienced the positive impact of Lean in their work.

This is an advantage one can use as a way to approach some of the problems outlined and that relates back to miscommunication.

Consequently, I am proposing that we adopt Lean methodologies to approach and solve many of the issues that are becoming more visible with the acceleration of our globalized economy.

Through the story of Boern GMBH, several more ideas on how to do this are exposed and I'm sure that many more will come from those who apply this way of thinking. I must emphasize that because there is no cookie-cutter approach nor a one-size-fits-all way to approach problems, I avoided being prescriptive with specific solutions, while providing the reasoning behind and the use of a few tools that could be very useful for a company like Boern. Those are based on my own experience and since every company is different, deep reflection and conducting a complete and proper analysis is indispensable in order to describe your unique current state—and make the specific changes needed to deal with the impact of globalization in each case.

Learning happens at the gemba, so you'll have to visit your own gemba to see things through your Lean eyes.

Furthermore, small and medium-sized companies are the lifeblood of many economies and frequently serve the supporting structure for larger companies. While scores of books and case studies reflect on problems and solutions for large companies, I find many are quite indifferent to the circumstances of small and midsized companies. Considering that a supply chain can only be as strong as its weakest link, it makes sense to pay attention to the successes and failures of those tiers and help find solutions that ensure they develop adequately in the face of globalization.

That said, I believe there is one common thread for companies to remain competitive in the current international setting, which is to ensure their teams are very focused and perfectly aligned so that their execution can be quick and at the same time effective.

Reverting to the excuse of miscommunication as a reason for poor execution is simply unacceptable if you consider you already have the knowledge and the skills to define, analyze, and solve a problem.

It's doubtful that globalization and the troubles it poses for companies are going away any time soon. If anything, I'm quite sure we will see more of it.

How This Book Flows

The book is built around the current situation at Boern GMBH, a German midsized automotive supplier of speed sensors used mainly in transmission applications. The company is fictional but the situations are very real, gathered from several companies I have been involved with and that have been exposed to some of the ugly truths of globalization.

While Boern did transform its manufacturing methods from its original way of producing by using Lean thinking and Lean methodologies, it did so only at the shop floor, where management saw notable productivity and efficiency gains. This effort was led by Johannes Boern, the current CEO of the company with the help of Kami Onata, a Japanese friend who was instrumental in introducing and providing the key ways Toyota had successfully applied in their production system.

Nonetheless, at Boern Lean thinking did not move beyond the transformation of materials into finished goods. It did not seep into the philosophies of leadership or management and consequently was not considered as a viable way to expose and solve some of the obstacles they encountered when they went global.

Like many companies, the prevailing mindset at Boern revolved around copying what was successful in Germany and adopting it in the sister plants internationally. The bigger problem, however, was the lack of understanding for the potential impact that working with people from foreign lands would bring.

As Johannes Boern became conscious that miscommunication had developed into a key factor, negatively impacting his operations and profitability, he realized he might be able to apply Lean thinking to solve those very same issues.

Chapter 1 provides a problem situation and the background and history of Boern GMBH. It allows the reader to see right from the start the process of communication and its important role and impact on how things get done in any organization. This chapter also exposes the increased role communication plays in global supply chains and the related costs we need to be aware of.

In Chapter 2, Boern learns about zero-based thinking and why their Lean initiatives should consider including Lean communication as a complement to their continuous improvement journey. Johannes Boern, the company CEO visits his logistics, engineering, and IT departments and exposes waste related to lack of coordination and miscommunication.

Johannes Boern then entertains the use of value stream maps to visually depict communication flows and the importance of sending a clear signal between every step of every process in Chapter 3.

Chapter 4 introduces ways to use standardized work in the process of communication as a means for Boern GMBH to reduce problems that stemmed from their globalization initiatives. At the same time, it sets the stage for the application of PDCA on the process of communication in Chapter 5.

Notes

1. Gemba which is sometimes spelled Genba is a Japanese word that depicts the place where things are happening, the actual place where an activity is taking place. This is the place where we want to observe if value is being added or where we can detect waste. The gemba is where one should physically be present to see what is happening. If you cannot be at the gemba, you cannot have direct observation and can only obtain a representation or an impression of the activity.

2. Korzybski, *Science and Sanity.* 1933. http://www.helford2000.co.uk/the-map-is-not-the-territory-explained/

3. Steven Spear and H. Kent Bowen, "Decoding de DNA of the Toyota Production System" *Harvard Business Review* September–October 1999.

4. The use of the term Lean to describe Toyota's production system is attributed to John F. Krafcik in 1988 in an MIT Sloan article http://www.lean.org/downloads/MITSloan.pdf. I personally first read the origin in Jim Womack's exceptional book *Gemba Walks* published by the Lean Management Institute.

5. Any language that is widely used as a means of communication among speakers of other languages. English, for example, is widely chosen as the *lingua franca* in the western world while Mandarin Chinese is widely chosen as the lingua franca in the Far East.

6. When we published *Lean Potion #9: Communication: The Next Lean Frontier*—Ashir, Diss LLC 2014, we wanted to share our initial notions of the use of Lean to improve the communication process. Our pledge was to continue to apply the ideas and concepts from that book and live by PDCA to provide readers new insights based on experience. The book you are reading is one more iteration of the PDCA toward a better way to share what we believe is a much-needed complement to Lean thinking and Lean management.

Chapter 1

Boern Industries

The $4 Million Crash of Zenssor211

In late 2013, Boern GMBH was forced to pull the plug on a program they had been working on for more than 4 years. They had had accrued a loss of more than $4 million which had already eaten into any possible financial maneuvering and a forceful decision had to be made. $4 million was a ton of money to lose for a company like Boern.

Looking back, many of the failures were now very clear and obvious but for Johannes Boern, the president and major shareholder of this very well-known automotive component supplier, it was tough to swallow. He had depended on his professional managers to drive and ensure a successful launch of Zenssor211, a revolutionary design of a speed sensor used in car transmissions. While at first he felt let down by his team, at the same time he reflected on his own lack of direct involvement.

Johannes, an engineer, had grown the company after he inherited the shares from his father who died very young. He had personally helped design and develop many of the products that helped increase sales and market share. The success of his company took place while they operated in the local German market with the direct participation of engineers he had graduated and grown up with.

In addition, all the suppliers they had subcontracted with were traditional German-based companies, many of them family owned and run. Business with them was transacted on a personal relationship basis: a handshake trumped any written contract.

Zenssor211 was intended to be a global platform and designed to support Boern's major original equipment manufacturer (OEM) customers in various continents. To meet this objective, Boern GMBH was in the process of establishing a couple of new facilities: one in China and one in the United States and hired a professional management team in each location. They also sent a small army of German expats to help with knowledge transfer issues and to represent the home team in foreign lands.

Boern China and Boern USA were responsible to identify and develop relationships with local material and subcomponent suppliers and integrate them with European components into the manufacturing and assembly process, to support the final product and deliver to customers in the region. While the US operation was for the most part up and running, they were still in the process of launching the first products in their Chinese facility.

Several components for the Zenssor211 program were assigned to the new global facilities. Unfortunately, prototypes and samples continually failed to pass some of the internal tests and the real costs of assembly and packaging were substantially above the projected estimates. This drove the Boern sales department to continually dance around the issues when customers asked for samples and prototypes.

Then, in June 2013, Boern's key customer GMBC,[1] the largest of the OEMs, presented an ultimatum and a final date to receive samples to use in their own internal testing and validation process.

But Boern could not deliver. The product was not ready.

GMBC sourced a competitor's product and canceled the business awarded to Boern causing the program to take a nosedive and a huge, embarrassing loss to the company.

Even though it was too late for this project, Johannes was determined to understand how they had gotten into this mess. He had to find out and make the necessary decisions to prevent similar future situations. A $4 million loss was indeed a very unfortunate wake-up call.

Boern GMBH: The Beginning

In 1910, Edward Boern, the innovative founder of Boern GMBH, used the horse barn on his property in Bavaria to develop a system of metal gears for a farm machine company in northern Germany. He was a skilled craftsman with great expertise in taking an idea, creating hand drawings, machining, and assembling the final product. He knew exactly what raw steel he needed and how to heat treat it to ensure long-lasting performance.

Edward had traveled from Bavaria several times to his customer in Spelle, in a distant, northern region of Germany to meet with the designers and assembly personnel of the most innovative harvesting machines being built at the time. Personal meetings afforded him time to review, take precise measurements, and ask all technical questions necessary.

When Edward produced the first prototype gears, he took them himself by horse and buggy to try them out directly on the customer's machines. He always traveled with a full set of tools that would allow him to adjust and make slight changes to ensure proper form, fit, and function of his gears.

Edward was Johannes' grandfather and aside from the many lectures he remembered from his opa,[2] he did recall that the biggest difficulty Edward had mentioned, was related to communicating with his German customers in the north. Opa spoke a local Bavarian dialect and had to make a tremendous effort to understand and be understood by his clients who only spoke a pure form of German.

It took face-to-face meetings to clarify and understand the expectations of his clients.

The company Edward Boern started as a craftsman, grew very quickly and once companies in Germany began to produce motorcycles and passenger cars, he was able to land voluminous contracts and thrive with his innovations and inventions.

From Germany to China to the United States

On a trip back to Germany, after visiting his Chinese operation, Johannes suddenly recalled what his grandfather said to him once: "When I was making the gear parts for the people in Spelle,[3] we were not the same people, by distance, food, or language—but they trusted me because I always showed up in person with the product and made it work perfectly."

Sitting on the plane flying over Asia, it dawned on him that he lived in a much different world than his grandfather did. Developing new products, sourcing materials, keeping up with technology, and making parts in many regions of the world required something opa had probably dealt with but in a minor way. Even back then his opa realized culture, language, and distance have an impact on your business.

Considering each of these factors meant that getting things done required additional coordination to ensure that every action, from every player, sitting in any of his global locations would flow in accordance to a masterplan driven from his headquarters in Germany.

The pilot on the flight interrupted the silence in the cabin with an announcement in Chinese and in English about some unexpected turbulence and to please remain seated with the seatbelts buckled.

Johannes was already feeling the turbulence in his company, and this moment sparked an idea in his head about the matter at hand—and what he had to do about it.

Would You Accept Right the Third Time?

Johannes Boern was now back in his office. Several years back, he had established a great friendship with Kami Onata, an experienced Lean advisor who had worked for many years at a key supplier to Toyota. Kami was Japanese and he had had worked in a few countries, where he had acquired a good sense for other cultures and different ways of management. His advice to Boern had been instrumental in improving the traditional ways in which the manufacturing processes had been originally set up.

Johannes wrote to Kami about the problems he was having and set up a time for a web meeting.

Kami: Very good to hear from you Johannes.
J: Likewise, a pleasure to talk with you again Kami. I hope all is well with you?
Kami: Yes, yes. I read your email and I think we should discuss some key things first. It is somewhat easy to forget a very basic principle that was coined by Mr. Philip Crosby about "right the first time."[4]

If one reads the principle from the perspective of quality, then the word "right" is what we tend to focus on. We would measure the conformance of a result against a pre-established standard and determine if it meets the expected quality. We could eventually make something right by correcting it, reworking it, repairing it. However, this would imply something was not acceptable that had to be repeated a second time or perhaps a third time. When we shift our perspective to cost, then "time" becomes the key word.

J: I heard the word "eventually" and this makes me upset. Eventually is not
  acceptable.

Kami: Correct, there is absolutely no way to recover lost time for free. There
  will always be additional, unbudgeted costs involved. In business,
  where time is money—this means that correcting, repairing or
  reworking are verbs that will end up contributing red color to our
  financial statements.

  Johannes, please take a look at some of the diagrams I'm putting
  on your screen. Take for example Figure 1.1 which depicts a typical
  two-way interaction: where person A is sending a message to person B. We assume A has the intention that his meaning flows to B,
  uninterruptedly and when B receives it, A's meaning is 100% understood by B.

When meaning A equals meaning B we might say that value is being added.

Suppose now that while A intends to make sure B understands the meaning of his message 100%, the two (A and B) are from different departments,
or from different countries. A is speaking too fast and says too many things
at once and they are team members from two different countries.

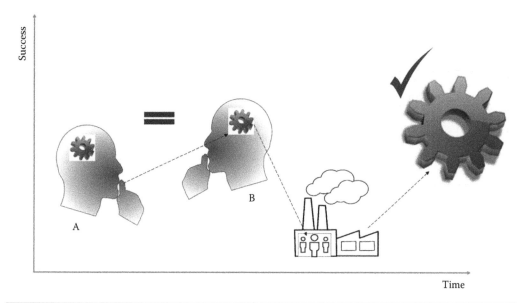

**Figure 1.1   The meaning person A transmitted to person B is the same. This is a situa-
tion where there is flow and value is added.**

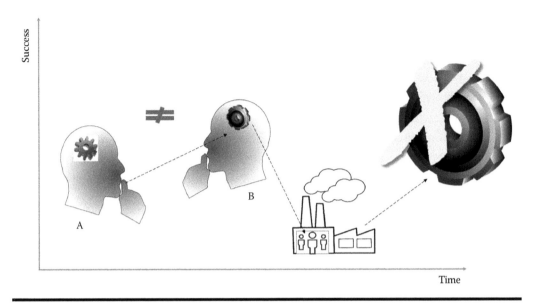

Figure 1.2   The meaning person A transmitted to person B is not the same. In this activity no value is being added. Stated different, waste is being created. This situation may trigger the production of incorrect parts, like a different gear from the one person A had in mind.

It is quite possible that in a scenario such as in Figure 1.2, meaning A and B will not match the first time in which case value is not being added and may potentially contribute to the creation of even more non-value-added actions, because communication is the source of every activity.

J: So you are pointing out that any task, any activity is preceded by people exchanging ideas or giving some orders and this is what triggers the way things get done?

Kami: For sure. But also pay attention to the time it takes to communicate clearly. In the context of our discussion about two-way communication, anytime that meanings don't match 100% the first time an exchange happens, a need will arise to spend time correcting, repeating, waiting, interpreting, translating, and repeating again….more waste.

In a perfect world, like in Figure 1.1, we can also make the observation that true flow is happening.

J: As you were explaining, I was making a hand drawing of how things were when my opa started developing the first products by himself. Have a look (Figure 1.3).

Figure 1.3   When Edward Boern, the founder of Boern GMBH started his business he could transfer the meaning of what he had in mind directly to his own hands and produce the gears he envisioned. He could directly adjust and fine-tune the parts by himself. No need to transfer the meaning to someone else. His ideas, strategy, design, and execution happened mostly with him. There was a direct connection between the ideas in his head and what his hands understood and executed. Any corrections and adjustments happened in real time, right there and then.

Kami: Your grandfather was able to execute things a bit faster and make adjustments in little time. But now Boern GMBH with the international sister plants has a different picture. Maybe looks a bit like this (Figure 1.4).

NEW OBSTACLES TO FLOW

As an organization grows, the goals and ideas have to be transmitted between the different layers of management in a way that they are 100% understood until these reach the areas that execute and get things done. In global situations things get in the way to the flow of meaning between the different layers represented mostly by obstacles such as language, culture, and distance. These factors pose a risk to the many projects required to accomplish the programs and new product development which in turn pose an even greater risk to the overall strategy of the organization. Paying attention to these obstacles that globalization brings is indispensable for the survival of the modern enterprise. There are more layers and now each layer presents a potential obstacle in between. Culture, language, and distance can affect the total amount of time a new project takes and the sum of the delays of a few projects could impact the timeline and success of a program or the development of a new product. If one or more programs or products are delayed and, for example, the competition gains market share, then there is a need to pay more attention to what might be happening, and what might be creating these delays?

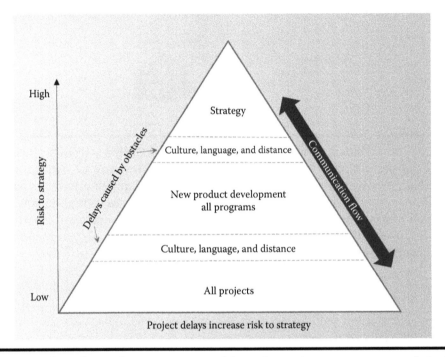

Figure 1.4 Obstacles to flow pose a new risk to the projects, programs and strategy of the company.

J: My dear Kami, I'm quite surprised, but communication is the common, underlying thread in each of these factors. This is not something I have been looking at and it is certainly not part of our budgeting.

Kami: You are not alone Johannes. Many corporations that have gone global make nice plans and cost calculations based on what they know. But when going to new worlds there will be also many unknown things and as these are discovered, they need to be considered in the calculations. So it is about continual learning and not only knowing.

J: I will for sure use many of our costly lessons learned to change how we are developing our plant in China which is not ready. We can still make changes. And correct things in the United States.

Kami: If you want, I will have some time to talk next week. For now I must leave to meet my old boss.

J: Great. Kami I will send you my updates and invite for another call. As always, Many many thanks!! Goodbye.

That evening, Johannes logged in to his LinkedIn to search for relevant articles where he might learn from other companies. While he did not really find anything really valuable, he did stumble upon this post.

ARTICLE: WASTE IN THE VIRTUAL PHONE CALL

I was sitting in teleconference the other day with my Lean hat on. There were participants from Mexico, Germany, and the United States and although English is the official language of business, I'm pretty sure that "solution" is not complete—with lots of room for improvement.

For starters, accents, combined with the speed of the exchange, for sure, not all words and meanings were clear to everyone. Then, consider technology—one party was still using an analog device and some of the messages were garbled. And then there was the native English speaker that felt very important using jargon, buzzwords, and acronyms expecting everyone on the call to be on the same frequency: "the drop dead date for the RTHD is EOB Friday so we don't have to double down and flounder. It's all low hanging fruit, and if you have to jump through hoops and burn the midnight oil……."

So sophisticated AND…. so inefficient.

What I heard several times: "please repeat," "please get closer to the phone," "what do you mean?," "What is RTHD?," "can you translate that please?," "hold on so we can explain that to the team" and again "please repeat."

With my Lean headset on, what I really heard was: waiting, rework, over processing, not right the first time, wasted human talent—just like in the 7 wastes on the shop floor….and about 40% of the meeting time was spent on these non-value-added activities.

Four people, in each location (total 12) with so many other tasks to do—wasting the most precious resource that cannot be reproduced because once it's gone it's gone.

We might as well take it for granted: with globalization this type of interaction is not going away anytime soon.

Johannes could relate to this story. He had been on many international telecons in the past where similar situations happened.

Notes

1. GMBC is a fictional name.
2. Opa is the German word for Grandpa.
3. City in northern Germany known as home to early agricultural machinery companies.
4. "Quality Is Free" by Philip B. Crosby (McGraw-Hill Books, 1979).

Chapter 2

Boern Uncovers the Waste

Johannes Boern had followed a business formula that many companies do: setting goals and objectives based on the current state while managing expenditures through yearly budgets. His management team's assumptions were that the baseline for improvements and growth was set based on the current operation level of costs and expenses.

Improvements were, therefore, achieved when results were compared with the current, budgeted levels, and a positive change was achieved.

Johannes discussed and pondered with his managers at the headquarters, whether their original assumptions were adequate, considering the new business scenarios the company was working in, especially since they had recently established new plants in other continents. Unfortunately, after many discussions and conversations, thinking inside the box persisted and no real breakthroughs occurred.

Then an opportunity to see things from a different perspective happened.

He remembered his friend Kami had sent him an article[1] a few months back, which explained the concept of zero-based thinking. Johannes searched his email, found the article, and read it again, this time with the context of his current situation in mind.

As he read, he sat back to reflect on the new lessons in the content and jotted down the following notes in his personal notebook:

> In a nutshell, instead of perceiving the status quo from the known, we could instead be open to explore the possibilities of removing every waste from every activity by setting the goal to zero instead of a random "acceptable" number based on an "acceptable" budget.

Just by changing the way we think, the direction of our continuous improvement plan will drive a search for every possible opportunity to reducing waste in every activity. This was a more realistic direction for goal setting, especially considering the new challenges we are experiencing with our recent geographic expansion.

The difference in thinking lies in the fact that instead of just looking at the typical labor, materials, and normal expenses, we can change the focus toward reviewing any and all activities required to get anything done. This would provide an opportunity to truly see in great detail everything else that surrounds material and production flows, where we have really concentrated most of the efforts.

Now I could change the goal setting from driving in the direction of meeting our own self-made illusion: our fabricated budget. Instead, we can set a direction toward a concrete and absolute concept that everyone, especially engineers—could understand: zero.

I think my engineers and I know that the typical way in which a budget has been built over the years, is through our department heads gathering data within their own department and providing it to the financial team for consolidation. In a sense, we follow a very German way, very compartmentalized that resorts to little or no discussion between the different functional areas and departments.

Our manufacturing processes are extremely efficient and our inventories are at an adequate level. But there are probably many other costs that affect our balance sheet in a negative way that we don't include in our improvement initiatives. We have become complacent with the situation through arbitrary "allowances" for inefficiencies.

The worst thing is that the budget has created a blind spot which has prevented us from seeing some negative things, and we cannot see them—but they can hurt us. With the new chapter in our history, opening companies internationally, we have to change some of our ways.

Zero should imply that every dollar is needed and cannot be wasted and if every dollar has the same value, then every activity must come under our scrutiny.[2] We will use the idea of right the first time which resonates with the concept of zero quite well. Zero tolerance for waste, zero activities that we will not consider.

Johannes had developed quite an intuition about his business. His gut told him he should start looking at all the possible wastes that had crept into his balance sheet when his company went global. In his mind, he could see a huge army of employees, at different levels and in different parts of the world meeting, interacting, and communicating—and these were activities that needed attention.

Before his next meeting, he once again reflected on how his grandfather did many things on his own, while Johannes' teams depended on cross-collaboration and communication methods, emails, virtual conferences, technical drawings, and operating instructions and IT systems to communicate what needs to get done.

A NEW GLOBAL MINDSET

The actual experience and success leaders and managers have had over the course of their careers will tend to create a habituated perspective on how things should be done for success. Their minds will likely be programmed to act in certain ways based on previous situations and they may excel in reducing costs, improving quality, and meet budgeted numbers.

These executives have a good chance of continuing with their relative success if they are tasked to operate in a similar context where the types of problems they encounter are similar to the ones in the past. However, these same executives can be detrimental to an organization that wants to stay competitive when they are operating in a context and circumstances that differ substantially from the one they are accustomed to.

In the stories in this book about Boern GMBH, none of their managers or the executive team had faced the types of problems that are typically inherent to a global enterprise. Their success was mostly based on their organic growth in Germany and their technical competence.

Meeting the budget had been a key corporate value, set as a priority by Johannes Boern himself when he became the company president. Everyone in his organization had accepted and adopted this way as the only right way of working.

This very same core value, which had very positive results in previous years, may have contributed to the current losses Boern was experiencing. Circumstances changed, the context changed, and the rules that worked before would also have to change.

The map did not reflect the new territory.

IT Systems

Johannes Boern had read the story of Airbus Industries and how due to a huge miscommunication problem, they ended up having to delay the launch of their first AB380—at a massive cost of more than $6 billion.

Although there were intercultural issues and language issues between the key players from Germany, England, France, and Spain—their misunderstandings caused further problems between two critical design platforms.

While the French team was using CATIA 5[3] for their design work, the Germans were using an earlier CATIA 4 version. Unfortunately, while the two platforms were related, they essentially did not speak the same language and the output produced by each did not match, causing the teams from different countries to produce flawed and conflicting designs. Thus, the first AB380 plane did not take off on schedule and the rework that ensued for more than 20 months cost the company a fortune (Figure 2.1).

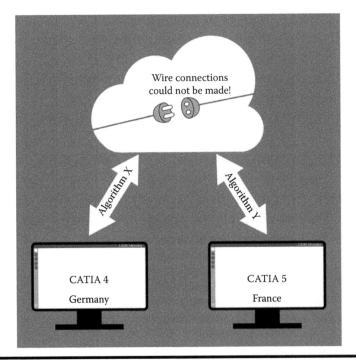

Figure 2.1   A misunderstanding happened between two IT systems because they did not speak the same language.

Johannes and Enterprise Resource Planning

When Johannes returned to his headquarters office in Germany, he immediately called his continuous improvement team and started a conversation about the types of waste and costs he thought were greatly affecting their company—and that were associated with their global efforts and communication.

Boern GMBH had invested in a new Enterprise resource planning (ERP) package with the intention to use it in a centralized way and to make work across his global facilities more efficient.

The implementation was expensive, lasted many months and was led by a local German team along with Boern's internal functional areas and their IT department.

The original business case for purchasing the system had been justified by reducing the amount of manual calculations, decreasing data entry time—but most of all for improving the reliability of the data and the accuracy of their reports. The time saved would create available time for the design and development of new products and processes.

They were looking for clear, precise, and timely information so that day-to-day decisions could be made efficiently and that every business unit could be on the same page at any given time.

However, based on the information he received from his IT team and his VP of Human Resources, the associated costs were on the rise.

It made sense for Johannes to go see the actual use of the ERP system himself. He would use the original plan as the standard to check against what was actually happening, just like he did many years before on the production floor.

MISUNDERSTANDINGS BETWEEN IT SYSTEMS

One of the main contributing root causes for the costly delay of the prototype Airbus 380 in taking off is attributed to the fact that the outputs of the two CATIA versions did not share the same meaning. While the newer CATIA 5 had an algorithm that accounted for the loss of total wire length in each curve on the fuselage, as well as the curvature of one wire bundle going over another, CATIA 4 did not automatically account for this factor—therefore, the resulting total length of many wires measured shorter than the required length to reach and make contact with the connecting wires between fuselage parts. IT systems, like Catia, have become extremely helpful tools for organizations and have mainly been adopted to improve business processes.

While, in general, we can say this is a good goal, many IT systems mostly mimic business processes and are programmed to automate steps. In some cases, because of programming limitations, implementation budget constraints, or system design restrictions IT systems are imposed on business processes which often drives the users to circumvent the "standard" way to work.

The Visit to Logistics

Central logistics had their office close to Johannes' and he took a short stroll to talk with the VP in charge. After he explained what he was looking for, they walked to the area where production control people sat all day in front of their computers and attempted to provide their production and procurement teams with the correct assembly schedules.

This team's role was to receive the customer signal, process it, and translate it into a schedule for the production and procurement areas.

He approached Helen, one of the logistics' teams' most experienced person and asked her to comment how things were going, how the ERP system contributed to her work, and if she perceived any problems. He asked for frankness and that his intent was to figure out what processes were not in line. Johannes made clear he was not interested in finding blame with specific individuals.

When Helen glanced at the VP from behind her two large computer screens, and got really serious, Boern could foresee the conversation was going to be revealing.

As Helen explained: "the ERP package does not always match some of the customers' software and the interfaces that were supposed to be online by now, are not working 100%."

Helen pointed Johannes to her screens.

> This means that incoming data, has to be downloaded and verified against other information that comes in from quite a few customers by email and other IT systems.
>
> I have to convert the ERP files and paste the values into a homemade Excel program someone in IT has written for us.
> The program compares the ERP figures with another data base and provides a calculation which I must then input manually back into the ERP platform.

Quite surprised, Johannes reflected: "This is different than I thought. The original plan was that the customer would send their signal electronically to our ERP system which would in turn translate the data and provide a build schedule to the production department. That at least was the standard we had envisioned and signed up for when we invested in the ERP package."

Now I see we often have additional handling, conveyance, rework, waiting….. and all are extra costs associated with the objective of transmitting accurate and timely information to the next link of our internal supply chain.

Helen, it is quite clear that you are committed to doing whatever it takes to get the job done and to satisfy your external and internal customers. But we will have to review this situation and get back to our original plan.

"Herr Boern," Helen responded, "I do all of it this way because the system drives me to do it so. I have to work around it."

Nonstandard Processes

GOOD INTENTIONS BREAK THE STANDARD

Where a standard way is not clearly defined, understood, and adopted by all, people will always find other ways to get the job done. Workaround systems tend to pop up when individual operators think they are solving productivity issues by adapting individual temporary solutions, convinced they are doing the right thing for their company.

As Johannes later found out, the practice of reworking the information from the ERP system was widespread and common in the department, where Helen worked with seven other planners. This meant a possible sum of many hours of lost productivity. He would, therefore, commission his Lean team to find out and determine how to approach the matter and, at the same time, understand how this waste was tied to the bottom line.

But Johannes also got very concerned that the original plan to ensure the accuracy of the information could not be guaranteed: people were actually manually entering data back into the main ERP—and this offered the potential for incorrect, inaccurate data due to human error. One small error such as a duplicate entry or a wrong decimal point entered into the virtual computer environment could contribute to much bigger problems in the material world: overproduction, too much inventory, or missed deliveries.

Globally, the other plants both in the United States and in China were tied to the central ERP and unfortunately had to use similar external subroutines to be able to "clean" up the data and communicate accurate details to their local production.

Johannes wondered if in fact during the initial analysis phase with the ERP supplier, it was clear that not all customer systems could communicate effectively with theirs. Not speaking the same language and without an adequate interface, more problems than expected would be created.

A similar situation was happening in the United States and China plants.

The cost analysis has shown that more than 20% of the time estimated for their total production planning and control team went to non-value-added activities and when multiplied by labor costs alone corresponded to hundreds of thousands of yearly dollars lost to waste.

And as we will see, the ERP system was not the only IT system that Boern found opportunities with.

Johannes Visits Engineering

Naturally, Johannes had a special relationship with his fellow engineers. His visit to the technical area was intended to be a more casual one and an opportunity to vent about what he was seeing in the other areas of his company.

Not surprisingly though, during his conversations with the engineers, he was made aware that they too were not following a standard and yet another area with uncharted waste surfaced.

Engineering Waste

The development team had grown quite accustomed to their existing home-grown document control system. The intended purpose of that system was to provide everyone in the company, including the organizations abroad, the latest revisions of any drawing, standard, and specification for each and every development and working process at Boern GMBH.

When the central ERP software was being developed for the company, it was intended to include a new document control module. The engineering department provided many important and critical details to the developers of the new system. After so many years of dedication by Boern's engineers, they knew too well that not respecting such level of detail could leave an opening for nonconforming parts to be produced.

However, even though the outsourced ERP developers were software engineers, their focus was on financial accounting and their background was more linked to bookkeeping. The two teams did not speak the same language. The criticality of the details communicated to them by the engineering team at Boern was not effective.

Thus, many details were disregarded by the system developers and the ERP package was launched leaving the new document control system, and Boern GMBH exposed to dangerous gaps.

In an attempt to ensure that the data were safe and no distorted information would flow to anyone at Boern, the engineering team decided to continue using their old, legacy platform, and manually transferred details that were left out, back into the ERP interface.

Besides the risk of error in manual data entry, keeping a redundant system was not in the original plan of the company. The IT department had to provide support and maintain the old code and software that the legacy system was based on.

This added up to excess hours booked to sustain an additional system on top of the manual data entry hours paid to engineers.

Johannes addressed these issues with Hans, the department head and the following was their short exchange:

Hans: der Teufel steckt im Detail, you know Johannes the devil is in the
    details, and without attention to these, we can get into deep trouble
    with our customers.
Johannes: Agreed Hans, but the details you are referring to cannot super-
    sede the good of the company. Even the most careful data entry
    person can make a mistake that no one would detect.
Hans: We were trying to protect the company. But I understand and can be
    available to help find a better way and fix this problem.
Johannes: Great I appreciate it. By the way, you make big bucks and
    deserve it—but the time lost to data entry is very expensive for
    the company, especially when you should be using every minute
    toward developing new ideas and improvements for our speed
    sensors.

Johannes Reflects

Johannes Boern blamed only himself for not staying close to the action. The devil in the details that Hans had referred to certainly applied here where an expensive state of the art ERP system could not guarantee data accuracy nor communicate effectively with the internal teams and customers. A human interface was still needed and a redundant legacy system was still in use, intended to ensure accurate information would be conveyed to everyone in the company.

While many of the issues he encountered were not low hanging fruit, nor easy to solve, he was convinced that doing things right the first time had been violated and now his company was paying dearly and losing valuable time.

After meeting with his team, everyone realized that in addition to the initial problems uncovered during Boern's investigation, it became clear that the accuracy of the information the plants in China and the United States were receiving had to be reviewed and challenged.

Although in too many meetings, there had been many previous discussions about this possibility between the logistics departments from each location and the headquarters in Germany, the problem was never clearly defined, nor understood by a predominantly technical team—and therefore due attention was not paid.

In a nutshell, the resulting data being conveyed from the central IT system to the different areas and global plants, potentially contained distorted or incomplete information which were contributing to the creation of many other wastes. Clearly, some of the prototypes that had to be built in the US plant had in fact failed due to the use of an incorrect engineering revision.

Johannes Boern knew he was on to something and he recognized he had to continue his personal visits and reviews in order to catch up from the lack of attention he had directed to his processes. He suspected that there were additional issues associated with the transfer of information between departments and continents. He returned to visit his technical team the following week.

A Call with Kami

Johannes felt compelled to call Kami and chat with him. He now knew for sure they had deviated from the original course of excellence and success and needed some coaching and, perhaps, a bit of reassurance. He called Kami and found him right away:

Kami: Well Johannes, I have to tell you I have seen this before with some other companies that have also entered the international arena. And the problem seems to be mostly self-inflicted, because of the way of thinking. Your company has been quite successful and has followed certain ways to overcome obstacles and become a great automotive component supplier. And this kind of success feeds on itself because we see that we are doing well, then our ways must be good. And they are. But this does not mean that when an important circumstance changes, you will still continue to be successful by following the same ways. Do you follow?

Johannes: Yes Kami, I think so. Also our "ways" as you say have been followed from generation to generation. My grandfather set some techniques and traditions that we have tried to follow and they have actually worked well. Even the new people that we hire have been trained to do things the Boern way. I guess though that with the change to a global setting some of our "old" ways might not be the best? Or maybe not enough?

Kami: I think that success can sometimes create a blindness Johannes because it keeps us from seeing other things that can be valid and useful. And also it can blind us from seeing a change that can actually impact our business. We sometimes do not reflect on the reasons we have been successful and if there is a change in those reasons, we can be alert to how to deal with the change. This is also an opportunity to learn from things we did not notice before.

Johannes: As you are saying this Kami, it is now becoming clear to me that while we were just in Germany, we could handle everything very quickly because things were close. And this factor, to be close, also allowed to have discussions with anyone in the company at any time—which allowed us to understand and clarify things. By having things clear to everyone, then things were easier to get done and usually they got done correctly, and on time. I think we really didn't, as you say, pay attention to this factor, and now it is popping up in many places in our company. There is a lot of problems with the way we communicate and it has hit our bottom line very hard.

Kami: Yes, Yes. Many people tend to take for granted the fact that when we have a shared language and a shared space the execution of actions flows much better. That contributed greatly to your success in the past. I also know that the German language is very precise and this means that instructions and knowledge is transmitted accurately. Germans can follow the thinking Germans in most cases. This is good for the speed of execution, because it can keep a steady, predictable pace until a project is finished. So, this is an important thing to recognize because it points to the opposite situation, where the transfer of info and knowledge is not so exact and quick. This might then be part of the problems and the waste you are seeing in your business today, and the slower speed of execution. One good thing about this Johannes is that when you know this and pay attention to these factors, then some solutions can be designed and tried out.

Johannes: It's obvious now that past success does not guarantee future success. I will have to make some notes. I want to make sure all my employees realize this too and that we can raise the awareness of the need to ensure clarity and understanding when we are communicating between people from different countries.

Kami, when would it be possible to meet? I think a face to face with you can be of great help. What is your schedule in the next weeks?

Kami: Yes Johannes, I will be in the US for a conference this coming 20–21 of May, so if you are going to be around I'll make the time.

Johannes: Perfect. Please send me the details. I'll plan to travel and meet you then. Thank you!

Drawings

To further grow the China and US facilities, Boern GMBH had put a plan together to transfer to those countries a portion of the business they had in Germany.

The company had numerous models of sensors: some low-volume and other high-volume ones.

They decided to transfer the bulk of the low-volume models to the United States and a small number of high-volume runners to China. Many of the low-volume parts were service or aftermarket parts and it made sense to localize these in one single plant. These would be opportunities to ramp up the new Boern facilities.

An assumption had been made and that everyone agreed was very realistic: because the parts had been already running for so many years, the production processes were mature, fully developed, and standardized.

Therefore, they would just "copy paste" the German processes into the US plant.

What Johannes Found

In total, 450 different part numbers were slated to be transferred to the US plant and teams in each country were established to support the project.

In all, 250 part numbers had been transferred over a period of 9 months and something did not make sense: considering that the parts were all well known surely by now all the parts should've been already running in the US plant.

The team in the United States had established a process to review the drawings of the parts in conjunction with their procurement team who sourced compatible components and materials from local suppliers. While originally they estimated that approximately 10–12 models could be reverse engineered for US production, they encountered many unexpected problems.

Johannes showed up unannounced to one of the team's teleconference, scheduled twice a week between engineers, logistics, and purchasing personnel from the United States and Germany.

Most of the discussions were centered on two topics: problems with drawings and specifications.

He could hear the voice of the American engineering VP, Billy Franks talking about the last three drawings:

> ...so it may very well be that you know what those details mean to you, but it is truly not clear to our team from drawing AE4567 if the measurement should be taken from the base noted by letter G or if the correct total length is 35.7 +/− .02 mm. The drawing is very ambiguous. And the handwritten scribbles cannot be deciphered.

Then another American engineer requested clarification on the specification FRT-01 rev 2 that referred to a measurement method and asked:

> ...what is meant by: traversely to the left through *mittelpunkt?*

Following, the purchasing leader from the US plant asked:

> We have found a compatible US based resin for this part because
> the original one is restricted in the US. But when we tried injection
> molding with this resin the surface has a different shine than the
> one specified in the drawing…

Perhaps, the strangest thing Johannes heard in that meeting was with
regard to the amount of handwritten notes in German on a drawing and
how difficult it was to figure out what it said in order to get an accurate
translation. Apparently, this was not the only print where manual markups
had been questioned for clarification. Even the two expats assigned to assist
with knowledge transfer in the United States had been unable to decipher
many of the scribbles and some peculiar words.

As the meeting continued for another hour, Boern sat quietly taking
notes. He was trying to collect as many opportunities as possible to later
make heads or tails and grasp the situation.

What Are the Issues?

It was quite obvious that the management and the engineering team had
missed the mark with their considerations about transferring some sensor
models to their US plant. While the estimates and calculations looked quite
good on paper initially, the real picture was quite different and once again
some opportunities were beginning to surface that pointed to waste not
previously visible.

Clearly irked, Johannes asked to meet with his management team and
his continuous improvement leader and read them a summary of what he
believed was happening with the US transfer project:

> … Number one, the intention of our drawings is to convey an
> accurate and specific meaning to the people that read them. This is
> clearly not the case in many of our drawings. Number two, hand-
> written notes are only ok temporarily but the drawings have to be
> updated in a timely fashion with clearly printed notes. Number 3,
> the translations of our specifications are meant to ensure that oth-
> ers understand the intended meanings. I read a few translations
> and I think we may have to look for a better process to ensure that
> the English version of our specs is 100% clear for anyone.

He continued: …we are in the middle of what many of you call a hand off. If you ponder about what this truly means it has nothing to do with throwing a ball and playing catch. In reality this is about ensuring that complete knowledge is transferred clearly and completely to the receiving party. In this case the US plant is an integral part of Boern and therefore there is no reason to omit any information.

It seems to me that we have forgotten that not every person knows what each of us knows. Because of this we then transmit the knowledge in ways that are incomplete, not fully understandable by others. I think the best way to change this mindset is for each of you to realize how the next person, receiving your drawings might interpret these. Walk in their shoes, see it from their perspective.

To be honest, I think that our drawings have never been perfect and I remember the many questions our manufacturing teams used to ask to clarify exactly what was intended by the design engineers. The advantage we had was that we were all close in our physical distance but also culturally. We took all that for granted.

Either way, it is the responsibility of our team in Germany to ensure that we provide any and all info, in a very clear way to our US and China team in order to ensure the success of Boern GMBH.

And I want you to think continuous improvement, ask yourselves: what must I do to make my drawings fully understood?

Does anyone have any suggestions?

The meeting room got quiet, and Johannes knew he had been strong and direct and that people would probably come by later in person to share their ideas.

The Waste

While Johannes spoke, Britta, the continuous improvement leader had been taking notes, got up and wrote some ideas on the dry erase board in the meeting room.

The first word she wrote was: Waiting.

Although the teleconferences associated with the transfer project lasted an hour, many tasks were then left for engineers and purchasing personnel to clarify or find out in order to report back in subsequent meetings. The transfer process of the particular part number was virtually stopped while new information was gathered, drawings were updated, decisions made, etc. things accumulated as work in process.

Then she wrote: Rework.

Many drawings had not been updated to reflect the correct way to manufacture the specific part. As the production was being done in-house, in Germany, many people knew how to make the parts and notified each other verbally about the changes or updates. Knowledge was transferred locally between people but not standardized for everyone to understand it.

In addition, the translations would have to be checked and in several cases redone in cases where it was clear that they would not be understood. A technical translation team would be required to correct the current versions.

Excess processing was the next word she jotted down.

The amount of communication back and forth between the teams to coordinate the transfer was truly unimaginable. Between six and seven people from each country had to meet twice a week for an hour to talk about and convey the issues and details in each drawing or spec that had to be clarified, updated, or corrected.

Not only was this conveyance time seen as wasteful but the fact was that the teams comprised of very creative people that were being bogged down with a process that was about cleaning up instead of innovation and improvement, a direct example of yet one more type of waste: wasted talent.

Johannes was somewhat surprised but at the same time excited that Britta was also able to grasp the wastes based on what they had all learned and applied in their manufacturing processes. He asked her to put together a summary of the wastes she saw in the process of communication in a way that could be analogous to the seven wastes everyone was aware of based on the manufacturing process.

The meeting ended and Johannes walked back to his office to continue his investigation and to add the view of some of his people in the new plants.

A Call with George Richards: The US Plant Manager

Johannes had made a mental note to make a personal call to George Richards, the plant manager in the United States to discuss the situation with him, hoping to figure out ways to improve interactions between the head-quarters and the US plant. Certainly, he thought there could be some good ideas from the people that were actually involved in the daily work across the Atlantic.

The call was clearly an eye opener for Johannes, who had not really expected any of the issues that Mike brought up.

Johannes had spent several weeks with George in America and they had already established a relationship where Johannes had accepted being addressed by his first name.[4]

After a quick greeting, the conversation started.

Johannes: George, we have obviously missed some things in our planning and there has been an impact to our results. We know there is no one to blame, in fact that could only be me. Nonetheless, I wanted to hear from your side—as a professional manager—what you have observed and what we have to do to change the way we interact—I mean from the headquarters with our international locations.

George: This is a good call Johannes. I've been wanting to write you but it's always better to talk. I think you and I have a few things in common, but most important I think is the fact that we have had a good amount of Lean education and perhaps it's good to use that way of thinking to figure out the gaps. If it's ok with you, I'll use some Lean analogies to discuss what I've observed.

Johannes: I'm not sure about the Lean analogy, but yes I want to hear your analysis.

George: OK, Johannes. Thanks! I wanted to note that the relationship between the headquarters is lacking respect. And I will clarify that this is in the sense of respect for people when we directly involve them in the process of continuous improvement and to solve problems. I have to say that this is an area where we have experienced a normal bias of the German associates feeling comfortable just meeting with their German colleagues to solve problems. The people actually doing the work are not asked to participate and as you know from your own plants in Germany, they are the ones that can bring true knowledge about what is happening, they are the ones doing the work. Johannes, I think you can follow the analogy of Lean and what we learned about the respect for people?

Johannes: Yes, George thank you for bringing it up this way and explaining—because when I heard 'respect' I was just translating this into German, thinking of a different context. I'm taking notes by the way and we can use your observations to design a plan to fix some things. Please continue.

George: The next issue is perhaps more specific, in regards to the way the part drawings, the work instructions, and several specifications were provided in a bulk manner. By this I mean that every document was probably sent to be translated in a batch process. And there was no opportunity for feedback from the customer to ensure the translations would be effective. In this case, my engineers were the customers and as we saw, many translations were not clear enough and it was not possible to follow a coordinated process. But they had no way to provide feedback to you while the translations were being made. A better way might have been to use a Plan-Do-Check-Act (PDCA) approach and have the customer check the end results of the translations to see if these were usable and if some adjustments could be made.

Johannes: This is a very good idea George. And PDCA could work quite well in this sense. I guess we just thought that the translations would be perfect and would be understood by everyone in the same way as our guys did. I've made a note for the next time we have to do this. I know for example that for us Germans and the Americans we use exact words to communicate but perhaps this is different in China. I have experienced where one word can mean many things, so we will have to improve on the work instruction translations and other documents in a way that they can understand exactly. But for sure we will do a PDCA with them on this and try out a few ways.

We have another twenty minutes on the call, if you have some more such ideas, I will be very happy to hear them from you.

George: Thank you Johannes. I think it makes sense to share with you also that the process flows that were provided by the headquarters to make the parts in the US were not helpful. I think the idea to copy-and-paste a process is not always good. If you consider that the part numbers that were chosen for US production were mostly low volume and aftermarket parts, we cannot build production processes exactly the same way as the ones for high volume. The reason for this is that low volume implies that there will be change-overs more often. If we do not pay attention, each changeover can create more loss to scrap because of startup parts each time we switch to another part number. And the material flow process will also be different because on many of these low volume parts we have different materials and these too will be supplied to the molding and assembly lines in smaller quantities. I think that on paper every part looks the same on a print and this can create the illusion that the process to make it will also be the same. So this has created a challenge for us here to design a process that can match the smaller quantities and make them in an efficient way.

Johannes: Wow, this really proves that the devil is in the details. And I also understand now why some of my engineers were very happy to choose those parts to send to America. I think the productivity would have dropped here in the plants in Germany because the processes were already set up to run every part the same way. But it is clear the details were not brought to consideration. I have a feeling we have a problem with the way we estimated the costs and the prices of the low volume parts. It seems that there will be higher costs and we cannot sell these and lose money. Have you looked at this Mike?

George: Actually Johannes, this was a point of discussion with Juergen, our controller, before we sent the price quotes to some of our local US customers. Specifically, for the aftermarket parts because I know these command a higher price in the market. The supply chain is different and the clients are different, more like supermarkets and retailers that don't behave like the OEMs. So for example our part # GF-0321, when it was a high runner for Chrysler and VW it only cost around $8.00 but the same part is sold in the US aftermarket stores for $48 bucks. Which means we can ask for a better price. Juergen was not in agreement at first, but we actually sent a trial quote to one of the buyers at Aftermarket Depot[5] and he did not even flinch, he accepted our offer and placed an initial order. In summary, every situation is different and we should try to avoid cookie-cutter solutions.

Johannes: Good George. I'm glad you took the initiative in this matter and that Juergen saw the opportunity too. At least on this program, we might end up making a better margin and make up for the losses we have taken on our delays and the Zenssor211. I have learned a lot from our conversation today Mike and I will certainly drive some changes in the ways we do things. I have to go to a meeting now but I do have another topic to chat with you about that I think is something you can probably help with. It is in regard to the way we interact in our organization, it's so compartmentalized and I'm beginning to think it is part of the reason we have such problems.

But I think you have some good ideas and I'll schedule a call at
3 p.m. your time to discuss with you. Thank you and until later.
George: Thank you Johannes, hope to talk again soon.

At 3 p.m., Johannes did in fact have a follow up call with George
Richards who brought up the topic of operating instructions, which had
unfortunately been taken care of in a much similar way as other details.

During this follow-up conversation with George, he found out about the
additional costs they had incurred in getting the operating instructions to
match the ones from the plant in Germany.

Boern GMBH had invested a large sum of money to start operations on
time in the United States but there had been unexpected delays of more
than 4 months that was impacting the project and the investment.

Here were the three top issues that came up in the conversation:

1. The complete operating instructions were not all in one document—
   there were additional appendices, loose specifications, and handwritten
   notes
2. Some information was only available by word of mouth from a few key
   experts who had traveled from Germany to train a team of supervisors
3. The translations from German to English were in many cases ambiguous and not clear

Many of these issues had been brought up to the trainers that came from
the plant in Germany but the solutions proposed had not been very effective
and the trainers returned to the headquarters prematurely.

George's team had tried to ramp up their production lines based on the
training and operating instructions. A lot of time was wasted on trial and
error, numerous phone calls to Germany, detailed measurements, adjusting, and measuring again. However, while they were able to mold parts and
assemble some final products, they could not maintain the level of consis-
tency needed for automotive components.

Johannes realized that this was one more factor that had negatively
influenced the development of the Zenssor211 prototypes and samples. In a
high-precision molding operation, work instructions needed to be followed
exactly as designed in every step of the process to ensure correct results.
While the instructions were clear and well known to the teams in Germany,
the transfer of knowledge to their US team had lacked the attention necessary to convey a clear message.

The waste created by sending incomplete or ambiguous information was now creating physical waste.

But Johannes also wanted to hear about the way George saw his team approach, in case this too was a contributing factor in the communication problems.

George Richards was a native of a small town in upstate New York. He was very direct and did not like to beat around the bush. So, he took the invitation from the CEO and told him:

George: Johannes, me and my guys see a heavy influence from the engineering department in everything that is done. Other areas in the company seem to receive less importance and focus. Like you, I'm also an engineer but many years ago, when I started my career in the auto industry we realized that to satisfy the customer, all areas had to coordinate and align their activities. Purchasing and logistics, human resources and manufacturing, and materials and engineering, for example.

We, of course, experienced numerous situations where one area made a decision on their own that created a lot of waste and disrupted the coordination, but at the end the customer was impacted. And this is when management and everyone agreed to work in a cross-functional way. Every function is important. Every function adds some type of value.

The key perhaps is to realize that there is not one function that can do it all and each is interdependent on the other, so a good way to maintain this balance in by designing your structure in a horizontal way, and clearly defining a cross-functional approach.

Johannes: Wow George, thank you for the clear explanation and for being open about it. Based on what we are seeing in our globalization efforts; this makes even more sense. I guess the knowledge and skills we have acquired as engineers really has not prepared us for such surprises?

George: The way I see it Johannes, we have focused on very technical skills which is extremely important and critical in the development phases of a new project or program. But to interact with the other essential players we have to also know how to communicate effectively. This means being able to express our abstract ideas and thoughts in a way that other people understand, because it is in our best interest.

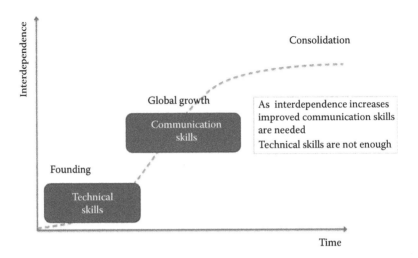

Figure 2.2 With globalization, interdependence between supply chain players increases, which in turn affects the skillset required by the players. If technical skills were sufficient at one point, today communication skills and intercultural skills must become part of what is required to work efficiently and effectively in the new gemba.

Otherwise, as we have already seen, the timeliness of our projects will be impacted negatively.

Johannes: George, I really do appreciate your insight on this. I've noted your comments and will include this analysis when we all sit to review all the points of our current state. Of course, we will do so in a cross-functional way so that every area can participate. This was a great conversation. Thank you very much and I will be in touch again (Figure 2.2).

Effectively Conveying Know-How

Operating instructions are the key procedures intended to communicate the steps required to obtain a specific result. When standardized, these instructions will contribute positively to the reduction of variation, ensure the reliability and repeatability of the processes, and to maintain high levels of quality.

They are also designed to maintain a safe environment for the operators.

In a nutshell, the know-how of the main plant in Germany had not been conveyed in an adequate way to the US team and this lack of, or under-communication, in turn contributed to unbudgeted costs and a delay in the ramp up.

The Cost of Rework: One Instruction at a Time

The engineers at Boern GMBH in Germany tried to provide their colleagues with the complete operating instructions and the know-how by supplying each and every document available to them in Germany.

The first thing that George Richards and his team did when he received these was to piece together each document and match it to a specific operation instruction. In most cases, there were loose appendices, copies of scribbled notes, and separate booklets with technical specifications.

The German team collaborated to achieve this first step and the task was done in just a few days. They were instrumental in figuring out the handwriting and assisted in getting those notes typed into an MS Word document.

While the teams pieced together all the documents, they read many of the instructions which had already been translated by the headquarters from the original German version into English several years before.

Unfortunately for the American team, a lot of the instructions were ambiguous and unclear. Some words were not really in understand-able English and the complete instruction was difficult to understand. This meant that it would be better if all the documents could be locally translated into English, for which George decided to outsource the documents to a couple of translation services, he trusted for their technical competency.

Following a PDCA and experimentation approach, he chose three initial sets of instructions to ensure the translations were correct and confirm with his German colleagues that all meanings matched and the instructions were understood 100%.

Again, the operation in China was brought up in all related conversations because of the way meanings flow with people from that country. At the very least, this was lessons learned that could be applied to the knowledge transfer to that country (Figure 2.3).

Details Emerge

George Richards was instructed by Johannes Boern to provide him with the total amount of hours his team spent piecing together the information, the cost of the translations, and the time it took for these to be effectively done.

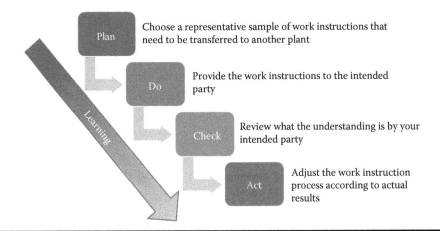

Figure 2.3 George Richards, the US plant manager, adopted the scientific approach by experimenting, via PDCA, in search of a better way to ensure the intended work instruction's meanings were clear and unambiguous.

He was disappointed with the way these things were being handled but at the same time realized that the main focus of his teams was on the technical aspects of his business, with little to no focus on the problems arising from language and distance.

A NEW USE FOR LEAN

When the word Lean was originally coined, it was tied to the word manufacturing and most of the work done started out in companies dedicated to the transformation of materials into finished tangible goods. Lean has come a long way and has reached critical mass and its being used to improve processes and create a better customer experience in the healthcare industry as well as in the financial and retail sectors. If communication is a process, and it helps us complement our work in continuous improvement, perhaps we can attach the suffix "communication" to the word Lean?

Boern's Eight Wastes of Communication

Britta, the continuous improvement leader, has asked to meet Johannes to share with him an initial concept of the wastes she could define in the communication process. She had made a rough sketch that she brought with her to show her boss (Figure 2.4).

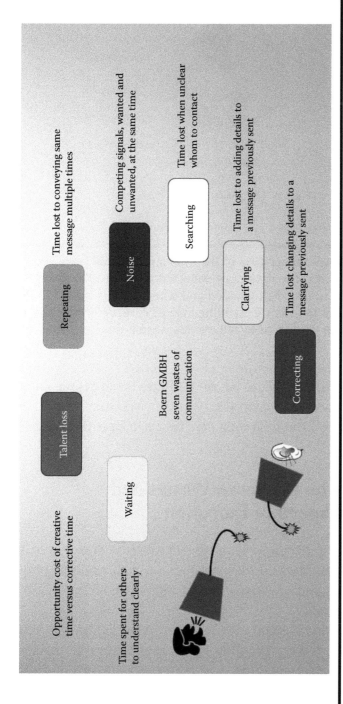

Figure 2.4 The Boern team represented most of the wastes they had identified in this initial illustration with the idea to create a parallel to the original seven wastes discussed in the Toyota production system. This was not meant to be a final depiction of the wastes they encountered in their communication process but it was a good first-pass image, and it served as a great way for people to see the relevance of each of their activities, including the transfer of information, ideas, requests, or any other transaction required to coordinate activities. In Johannes' mind, in every interaction between his team members, they could become aware of situations where value was not being added.

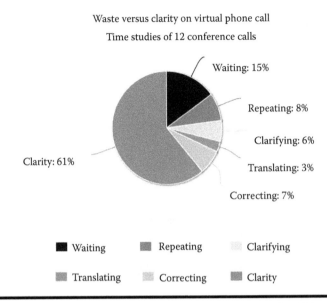

Waste versus clarity on virtual phone call

Time studies of 12 conference calls

Waiting: 15%

Repeating: 8%

Clarifying: 6%

Translating: 3%

Clarity: 61%

Correcting: 7%

■ Waiting   ■ Repeating   ☒ Clarifying

☒ Translating   ☒ Correcting   ■ Clarity

Figure 2.5 **This chart shows almost 40% of the time a virtual call is wasted on typical non-value-added activities. The data were collected at the gemba, sitting on the calls, and observing when value is being added and when there is waste. Challenge your team to establish what this metric might be in your case, determine the root causes, and then chart your next steps to reduce this wasted time so it can be redirected to better use.**

Britta had taken the initiative and sat on several virtual phone calls to determine the effectiveness based on the type of waste they were now focusing on and produced the following chart for her boss (Figure 2.5).

Johannes Reflects on the Seven Wastes and the Impact to the Speed of Execution

Johannes had learned the business from his grandfather who was truly a technical genius. He had followed the concepts and ideas closely and had been able to grow the company based on the incredible technical backbone the company had acquired.

Nonetheless, times had changed and as Boern reflected on the issues at hand and compared them with the times of his grandfather he realized that there was an important difference that had not been considered.

While Edward Boern had worn a local thinking cap, Johannes was for the first time, meeting the big world. The skills required to be successful were beyond the technical ones his team had in the past excelled at.

The collaboration needed between his global teams required a lot more attention in order to coordinate activities at a distance. Besides the technical skills, they would require intercultural and communication abilities.

He had taken for granted the speed of execution achieved while his company was only in Germany. One advantage lay in the German language and the exactness of words everyone understood the same way. From kick off to execution to success, the timelines were for the most part quite predictable. But now the speed of getting things done was being hampered by seemingly small and simple things.

Too often, his friend and advisor Kami reminded Johannes that "problems need to be solved while they are still small. This is when they can usually be addressed without a lot of energy spent. Once problems get big, the solutions can become complex and difficult to solve."

The seemingly small "soft" issues had been overlooked. While all the effort associated with the new plants was focused on the technical issues and the manufacturing activities, the activities related to interactions between people from different countries were being neglected.

Johannes realized that even if you don't see certain things, it does not mean they are not impacting your operation. He suspected that those same types of waste were responsible for the failed Zenssor211 program.

Now, he wanted something that could shed light on the issues they had missed and as well try to avoid these from impacting his future plans. As usual he liked to contemplate any available ways that Lean could provide, considering he had a trained staff with proven results in the manufacturing areas.

"In order to make those hidden issues come to the surface," he thought, "perhaps we can adapt the process of mapping the value stream of the activities we are not paying attention to—and at the same time determine if each activity is adding value, or not."

He looked for his Lean leader and started the discussion on how value stream mapping (VSM) would be used in this scenario.

Notes

1. Zero Based Thinking Illuminating Opportunities, Guiding Improvements. Performance Solutions by Milliken. http://hse.flemingeurope.com/webdata/3039/Milliken%20white%20paper.pdf.

2. Origin of the word scrutiny: Late Middle English: from Latin scrutinium, from scrutari "to search" (originally "sort trash," from scruta "trash") Oxforddictionaries.com.

3. CATIA is the acronym for computer-aided three-dimensional interactive application, which is a CAD/CAM computer-aided design, manufacturing and engineering software suite developed by Dassault Systèmes, a French company.

4. Using a familiar, first-name approach in the wrong situation could be insulting and should be avoided in business and social dealings with most Germans, who tend to be more formal and reserved than people in some other cultures when conducting their personal and business affairs. Expect some kind of acceptance before you address someone informally.

5. Aftermarket Depot is a fictional name.

Chapter 3

VSM: Seeing the Waste Globalization Dropped on Our Doorstep

In the book *Learning to See*[1] Mike Rother and John Shook provided Lean thinkers a simple, yet effective way to depict the whole value stream required to manufacture a product. Their book served as an introduction to the VSM methods Toyota was using.

In a nutshell, they explained that where there is a product that a customer is requesting, a value stream exists and by using VSM and mapping the stream, one can see and determine where value is being added, from the customer's perspective. The authors also clarify that at Toyota, people map out three flows: information, materials, and processes (Figure 3.1).

While Boern GMBH had in fact used VSM when they first started their Lean journey, they had not updated nor set out to map the current state, where the important changes they were experiencing with their incursion into the global arena could be revealed.

In fact, they assumed that the value streams would be the same based on their thinking that the manufacturing processes would be copy pasted into the new global facilities.

Once again, Johannes Boern decided he would have a chat with his friend Kami and pick his brain to get some ideas from him.

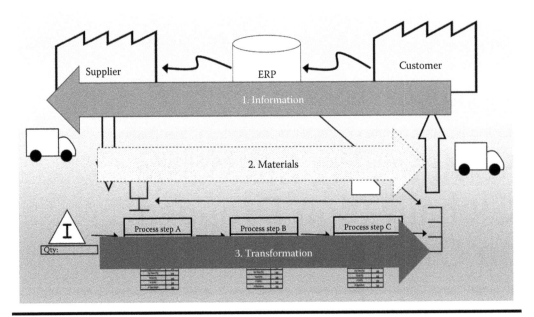

Figure 3.1 The three numbered arrows represent the flows required for an enterprise to produce value for a customer. While most books and instruction on Value Streams focus on the materials required for production and the physical processes, arrows 2 and 3, in my experience, a lot of non-value added activity originates and is triggered by what is contained in arrow number 1. Why do so many pay the least attention to this stream?

Learning to See the Other Activities

Johannes: Hello Kami, It's been a long time since we last spoke. How are things with you? Your family?

Kami: Thank you Johannes, all is well and you?

Johannes: Yes. Thank you for taking my call. I wanted to share with you some detail issues I saw in my company, that have created unexpected costs, and delays in our projects—and wanted to get some advice and insight from you. Specifically, we want to be able to see some of the issues that were invisible before, but that we know are affecting us. Can VSM help? What can you tell me about this?

(Johannes provides Kami with the background and situation, mostly related to the ERP system, the drawings, and work instructions. Kami listened attentively.)

Kami: Well Johannes I have to tell you; you are not alone in the situation. The past years I have visited many companies and the truth is they are standing still, not moving their thinking when using some of the methodologies of Lean. But many of these have had a similar shift like you, taking the company to another part of the world and this is a big change. I will explain something about value stream maps.

Traditionally, most of your focus has been on the flow of materials into your manufacturing processes and out as a finished good to your customer. Much less focus is put on the stream that represents the signal from the customer—and this might have been acceptable in a world where the supply chain was a local type and perhaps amounted to tens or even hundreds of miles.

We often forget that the map is being drawn to depict the flow of a process meant to satisfy customer expectations—as expressed by the signal, they transmit to the supply chain and that it is that signal that sets off the other two streams. As you know, few people place enough attention to this stream, where things originate (Figure 3.2).

So, if there is a problem with the signal, like if it's not clear or not 100% understood the same way as the customer intends, it may result in setting off incorrect material transformation processes that will produce and deliver something different than the intended expectation of the customer (See example in Figure 3.3).

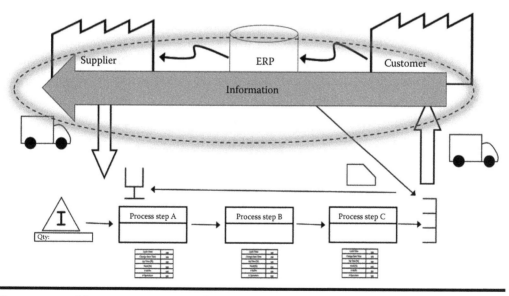

Figure 3.2 This arrow represents the customer's requests and expectations. What can happen to the material flow and the physical transformation process flow if the signal received is ambiguous and not clearly understood?

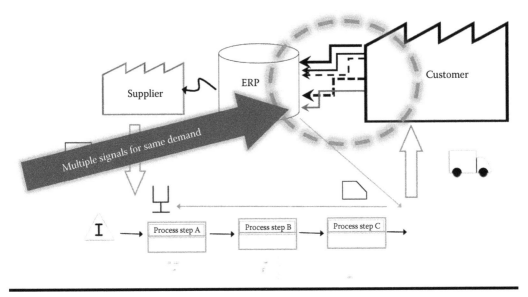

Figure 3.3 A company I worked with received negative delivery performance ratings from one of their main customers. After joint value stream mapping (VSM) sessions with the customer, the root cause was made clear: the customer was sending multiple signals for the same demand, thus creating a very confusing scheduling process for the supplier while at the same time impacting their own assembly lines. The demand was being sent by electronic data interchange (EDI), spreadsheets, emails, and even daily phone calls to "fine-tune" the schedule.

Therefore, now you have a lot more signals going on because you have a longer and more complex supply chain, which means more signals are being exchanged. And with every signal, there is a chance that the meaning being sent is not matching 100%. And as you mentioned, this is not only people talking but also emails and drawings and even IT systems that may not be compatible with each other.

It seems that from the three streams of flow: materials, production, and information, the focus today has to shift and consider the information flow with greater importance.

Johannes: This is making a lot of sense Kami. And as you were talking about the customer, I was a little confused thinking only our external clients but I now see how this is so related to our sister plants—they are our customer too.

Kami: Johannes, we must think about the signal we transmit to our own departments and that it is the signal that sets off their processes. This is for sure something that is creating a lot of extra costs and a lot of waste for you.

So Johannes, you want to restart the mapping process in your company again, it would have been good to do when you were planning your new plants.

Make sure you are drawing the map with all your teams—bring the issues to the surface, raise the awareness.

You know, in the exercise of drawing a map, involving members of the different teams, your people will be challenged to reflect on the way they each see a situation and can quickly interact with others to ensure the map is showing "reality" in the best possible way.

Think for a moment on the benefits of involving your global teams in the mapping process of your organization's steps in adding value to a product or service. This would in fact be a very appropriate way to bring to the surface any underlying issues that may be impacting or will impact the efficiency and effectiveness of your processes.

Remember it is people on the front lines doing the work, not your technology.

When I suggest drawing the map with the teams, I am including the leadership and upper management of the organization. Once a VSM shows an area where waste is being created, a visual image of the problem is etched in everyone's mind, understood the same way by everyone as a problem that needs attention. This is part of the beauty of visual representation.

Johannes: Kami, this is really good. I appreciate it.

So we agree, mapping is a great visual way to illustrate a situation with much greater clarity and allow for things we did not see before come to the surface. I think we will have to pay more attention to the way we receive and provide information in the longer supply chain.

Kami: My dear Johannes, that is correct. You have probably heard the phrase: the map is not the territory? And I think that like others, you may be living in an old map. The territory has changed dramatically. Manufacturing is only a portion of business today, so everything else that can be a non-value-added activity has to be revealed and dealt with. Supply chains are now where a lot of the transformation is happening and it takes a lot more coordination than before.

Kami paused for a moment and continued:

Actually Johannes, since you mention the word attention, let me give you an idea. Since in the past you were paying attention to the production part of your processes, it is quite possible you were leaving out some other areas of the company. I sometimes tell my people to be aware of the blindness that results when we make any decision, choosing one thing, leaving another out. And, we may call this prioritizing. But it has to be clear that there may be things that are not in your focus but have a mind of their own.

I like to call them Goryō, it's like a bad ghost in Japanese.

So, maybe one of the things you can consider and can bring those Goryō to the surface—so that you can see them and deal with them—is to revisit the mapping of your value stream and begin with the flow of information from beginning to end. You know, ghosts tend to dissipate when we shine light on them.

And don't forget that you have the internal customers, your own employees in every area of the company. So it's not only the external customer that has expectations that have to be satisfied. I hope you follow?

Johannes: Yes, Yes. This is a great way of looking at the problem Kami. As always I appreciate your insight. Will it be ok if I send you an email with the details I'm seeing? In case there are other pointers you can help with?

Kami: My dear Johannes. Absolutely. Under the condition that you share the findings when you start to map your processes again. I will learn a lot from the real things you find when you walk the new gemba.

And one last thing: when you come to Japan we will prove to you again that our beer is much better than yours.

Johannes: That is quite funny and will look forward to the process of evaluating the beers. And of course I will share our new mapping with you for sure. Many, many thanks and talk you soon. Tschuss!

Kami: Ah yes, Tschuss![2].

In the current situation at Boern GMBH, VSM can, as first step, bring some hidden issues to the surface by depicting them on a map. This first step does not in any way indicate how some of the non-value-added activities might be solved and these would subsequently require a Kaizen approach and root cause analysis to determine the potential solutions.

Learning to See the New Obstacles Created by Globalization

Johannes was now tasked to gather and work with his teams and attempt to use VSM to map out the current situation at Boern. What he was envisioning was to at least create the awareness at every level about the types of issues they would continue to encounter in their globalization plans.

The traditional flows of information, materials, and processes provided a clue. The word "flow" for him resonated with an uninterrupted series of steps from a start point until an end point. An interruption to this flow could be seen as an obstacle—and once identified, it could be analyzed, reduced, or removed.

Johannes requested a meeting with all the areas to review some of the different problems they had been discussing with regard to IT, drawings, and operating instructions and use these to define a way to draw these on the first part of their new current state map. He wanted to have this discussion before any mapping actually started.

And what are the potential wastes we are particularly looking for in our information streams?

Johannes asked each person in the meeting to comment what they were experiencing with respect to distance which was at least one factor he saw getting in the way.

These are some of the obstacles his personnel identified and are outlined in the following notes.

Distance

Hans—engineering: when we were working just in Germany, most of our suppliers were close by—I mean up to 150 kilometers. So, they were able to come to Boern and we would review all the specifications face to face. All questions got answered quickly and if any changes had to be made based on our specs, this was taken care of fast.

This factor alone meant that my team and I had more time available to be on the shop floor and take care of the technical problems. We were more efficient and used our time better.

I think now there is a lot of waiting happening. We have some suppliers in other parts of the world and sometimes it takes longer to clarify the specification issues.

Berndt works with Hans: I agree with Hans and also want to add that we depend many times on the samples and prototypes to evaluate and make changes to product or process designs. With the distant suppliers, this time is now many times longer and we must wait. And when the samples get in, we may have to stop another activity to review these. Since we are talking about flow, this distance gets in the way. It is an obstacle we did not consider before.

Helen—logistics: my issues are more about time zones. My area was used to working our normal hours based on the clients also having almost the same schedules we did. But now, we have to take care of situations with some of the suppliers and customers in other continents.

If the problems are sporadic, we can take care of the problems and move on. But often we have supply chain situations that have to be managed that can take several weeks to get back to normal. This means many of us have to stay here very late, or wake up very early and join telecons from our homes.

This takes a toll and after some time, we can have accumulated stress and not be able to take care of everything in a smart way.

Ernst—purchasing: for me it's about not being able to work face to face with people. Even communicating with fellow Germans, it's always easier when they are physically in front of you. Although we boast a very exact language, we have regional differences and also many immigrants. So body language, hand gestures, and facial cues will help us reach a shared understanding. Nothing ambiguous should be left for guessing.

The distance with our sister plants and some suppliers makes it tough to always have face-to-face meetings—and when we cannot, there are typically somethings not understood by all the same way.

Johannes—CEO: Thank you Ernst, thank you all. What I have noted from different conversations I've had, the distance between people reduces the level of relationship. We in Germany have little or no connection with our own colleagues in China or America. This is a normal human issue, but one that is affecting our work and our costs.

As an example, I want to point out that we are now using more statements about "those guys in China," which sounds very impersonal, considering "those guys" are also part of the same organization.

What are we mapping?

Understanding the pitfalls and the potential issues that could arise from geographically separated teams, we have an opportunity to make these visible by depicting them on our map. I'm always reminded of the point about being able to solve a problem only after it is actually visible—and VSM is a fantastic tool to make the invisible, visible.

In the case of physical materials or finished products on a VSM, distance might be alluded to through the use of lead times. Provided no obstacles get in the way, materials should flow unhindered and meet the stated lead times.

Similarly, the discussion that the Boern team is having is about the potential for incomplete, unclear, or non-communication between teams that do their jobs in locations that are geographically separated from one another. On the basis of comments from the different departments, distance is a factor that can impede the flow of activities such as: request, ideas, or decisions—all of which have to be transmitted and clearly understood before things done effectively.

Being able to see that the work to be done is going to be affected due to the physical separation of the people responsible will serve as a key component in any efforts to improve the performance of the supply chain. So, the details that may be noted on the VSM should relate to this with symbols that can ensure these details are clearly observable (Figures 3.4 and 3.5).

Language

English is most often selected as the language of business in global supply chain operations. Perhaps, the expectation is that when people from different countries are conversing in English, everyone is suitably understanding each other so well that when actions are undertaken based on the conversation, things will get done adequately, consistently, and according to the true expectation of the work to be done.

Nonetheless, Johannes realized this was just theory. In practice, language was causing many problems that even the best English speakers could not

Symbols to show time zones of your supply chain

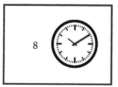 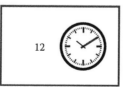

Figure 3.4   Consider adopting these symbols on your VSM, to account for multiple time zones multiple time zones that can and will affect your supply chains.

Symbols to show potential culture or language issues

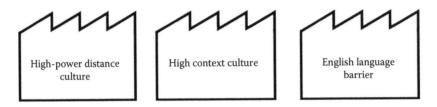

Figure 3.5   Consider adopting these symbols on your VSM, to account for people that will be interacting and that speak a different language and have different cultural behaviors.

get around. His team contributed the following comments about their experiences with the barriers posed by language:

Klaus from purchasing: I know there is due merit in selecting only one language, but many problems are still present when not everyone can speak it at the same level, for example: with accents it is difficult to recognize some words and then the meaning is lost. Last week, for example, we had a telecon with our plant in China, in English—and between our heavy accent and their accent we had to constantly stop and repeat, and even sometimes text the phrases so everyone can be on the same page.

Also, our colleagues in America often use idioms and buzzwords which are blurted just as decorations to sound special, but I get lost. Of course some people I think speak English too fast, then we have to stop to ask to repeat, slow down, etc. Time is wasted.

I sometimes get the feeling from some colleagues that they want to play games, and take advantage of our lack of English. Honestly, this makes me not trust them sometimes.

Katarina from HR: I am an advocate of using English as the lingua franca of business as it is important to agree on one common language to transact and obtain clarity. So, this means we must ensure that everyone receives adequate language training to reach a technical proficiency in English. I learned English in school but it's simply not enough to know the basic language, especially when business terms and specific technical or process topics need to be discussed.

To me it seems odd to see Boern GMBH spend enormous amounts of money on technical and technology solutions, software, and hardware—but have dismissed the idea of investing in language and intercultural training.

Hans from engineering: I want to just say that in my mind, language is also about the different software and IT platforms. For example, I heard from Helen in logistics that the ERP package we bought does not speak the same language as the customer's system. So, her team must act as a human interface and translate for our system. And I have that happening in my department with design platforms such as Catia and ProE. Sometimes the details don't match 100%. So to me, these systems don't speak the same language and we have to spend time to fix this.

Johannes—CEO: I agree somewhat about the English, but because of our new multicultural environment, it is imperative that people learn other languages to be able to have other types of conversations with counterparts in other countries. This shows respect, generates trust, and helps build relationships that can help get the job done in a more effective way.

I appreciate your comments and it is clear that we have paid too much attention to computers and technology while we have neglected the most basic and the most important technology to communicate effectively. We must have a common language to achieve a common understanding. Not achieving this as we have seen, drives a lot of waste and costs in quality, delivery, and lost customers. Our development is taking much longer than before.

This was the end of a very long meeting and Johannes could tell his team was exhausted. He thanked everyone for their frankness and comments and announced that they were invited for a follow-up meeting the next day at 3 p.m. He had asked an intercultural expert to provide a brief overview on national culture and how it might affect operations.

Uncommon Sense

Johannes went home early that day.

He recalled a recent situation one of his engineers had briefly mentioned and that tied with the topics of his meeting, and perhaps the next one as well.

Boern's first tooling lesson in China: One key initiative Boern GMBH had decided to drive was to develop injection mold tooling in each location. While the US plant was launching service parts with old production molds, the China operation was strategically established to supply high-volume parts to local OEMs, while leveraging local suppliers.

Purchasing provided the drawings for a first mold tool to several potential toolmakers and decided to award Naiting Industries the business. The engineering team had deliberately chosen a simple tool to try out, not really knowing what to expect.

The toolmaker sent the first prototype samples to Germany and after a few corrections, they provided a final set of samples, deeming the project ready.

The actual measurements and overall parts were good and matched the measurements very closely. What caught the attention of the Boern engineers was a small mark, like a score on one side of each of the sample parts—and this signaled something odd was happening in the process.

When photographs were shared with Naiting, asking what that mark was, they quickly replied that the score was "a streak left by the operator when he was helping to release the parts from the mold."

This was the surprise to everyone at Boern: why was there an operator releasing the parts? Nowhere in the discussions with the toolmaker had this come up.

The Boern engineering team had to dispatch two of their molding experts to China where they soon discovered that all along the toolmaker had been considering the use of an operator while Boern's intention was to use the tool on a fully automated machine.

While some of the reasons for this misunderstanding were communication issues, there were potentially some intercultural questions that should have been taken into account. For one, when the supplier in China responded "yes, yes we understood everything" it may have implied commitment to all the specifications for the team in Germany. Evidently not the same understanding for the supplier, even though the word "yes" was stated. In addition, the specification that was sent out to the company in China read: "To be molded on state of the art injection molding machines" which can mean different levels of technology in different countries. One of Boern's engineers made the comment about "they should have used common sense" and in fact they did—their common sense was different. In culture, my "common" might differ from you "common."

This event could certainly be used as lessons learned and help the team become aware of the cultural differences and their potential impact on business. At the very least, a personal visit to the supplier would have mitigated many of the misunderstandings and could have saved time and money.

For many, the word culture sounds very abstract and deep. When we travel on vacation, we can sometimes have fun noticing how people behave in different ways than we do. In business, however, the impact of differences can pose a risk to an organization's strategy. People from different cultures have been programmed from an early age to behave a certain way, to understand things based on their diverse upbringing and education.

The problem is that for the most part, we tend to be blind to this and act as if there are no underlying influences to the way we act and react to situations. Therefore, a key step in removing our blinders is to raise our awareness—and that of our team's—so that interactions can stand a chance to avoid misunderstandings and friction.

Johannes was certainly on the right track.

Culture

At 3 p.m. the next day, the Boern management team and a few other staff members sat in the main meeting room and greeted Brigitte, the intercultural trainer Johannes had invited to provide an executive style summary on culture.

"What is culture?" She started: "it is the social programming of the mind," according to Geert Hofstede,[3] a well-known expert on this very complex topic.

This may sound very abstract, so I will try to provide some concrete details and a way for you to relate.

Mr Hofstede gathered data from thousands of people from different parts of the world and came up with some definitions that could be used to understand the differences. The definitions are typically called "dimensions." And just like him, there were others, like Edward T. Hall[4] who also came up with some dimensions to help explain differences.

So, I will provide you with a few of these. However, I will ask that you help me with some situations you have encountered and that we can use as examples. OK?

The first one is power distance which really means how people behave when the leader is in the room. In a high-power distance situation, it is assumed that power is not distributed equally. This may be even more so in China, but quite different in America. Does anyone have an example from your work?

I see Klaus raising his hand.

Klaus: I'm not sure if this is relevant but when I visited our plant in China last month, the local personnel would not respond to my questions and would always defer to their boss. In fact the boss was a bit upset that I approached his workers directly.

Brigitte: Actually this is a very typical example. The typical Chinese are High Power distance, which means they show deference to their supervisor, it is not a culture of equality like we are used to. The typical German is more Low Power distance with a more egalitarian relationship between the boss and the subordinate. Thank you Klaus for the example.

It is possible in high-power distance environments that some ideas go unnoticed and not considered when too much respect drives a bit of fear. So, this is an important point to consider if you want to let all ideas be heard.

Now another dimension which is collectivism and individualism which are tied to the way a person sees himself or herself with respect to society. The Germans and Americans are more individualistic than the typical Chinese. We like to believe we can act alone, by ourselves or in a very small group—while in China, people recognize their interdependence on their larger groups. The family there is more extended than in our case. The key point of this dimension is the importance placed on the relationship between people and spending the time to create relationships can be more important for a person in China than it is for us.

Klaus once again raises his hand.

Brigitte: Klaus, I see you like this topic?

Klaus: Well, it seems I messed up then when I was sourcing for a toolmaker in China. I did not go there and establish a relationship with anyone. I just sent emails and documents, the same way I did in Germany. So maybe some of our expectations did not work out because of the lack of a better relationship.

Brigitte: Klaus, when you have a good relationship, there is a trust factor that builds up. Not only trust as in friends but also in the competency of the other person and their ability to get things done properly. So, this is a good example too.

Finally, I like one dimension from Hall which is related to the importance people place on the overall context versus straight communication. In Germany and in the United States, people communicate with words and depend on the use of words to exchange ideas, request things, etc. Mr Hall refers to this as low context, etc. But in

China, the emphasis is greater on the context surrounding an issue and the words are secondary and so this is a high-context culture. So, this means that even if someone in China speaks English or German very well, the words will not be enough for a complete meaning to be understood the same way by everyone.

Yes Katharina, you have an example of this?

Katharina: I have a lot of trouble speaking with my counterpart in China. She speaks English quite well, but I often find ourselves going around in circles defining and redefining a situation even though the concepts and the words we are used to using are very clear for us. I hear a lot of history and situations mentioned by my colleague in China, before a topic is understood.

Brigitte: Wonderful. That's it. Your example is quite clear and describes this dimension very well. Most Chinese will tend to go into very detailed descriptions of the circumstances and the context, trying to ensure that the whole picture is being considered.

I can see that the issue of culture is real in your case, as I have seen in many companies that venture into the international arena.

My task today is really to raise the awareness since Boern has been used to dealing Germans with Germans you can become blind to the way other cultures perceive us and our behaviors. And those perceptions can also create reactions that impact the work.

I also want to ensure that you realize the dimensions are not meant to show that one culture is right or wrong or better than the other. Simply each culture has its merits and we have to learn how to interact and learn from each other. One last item that I think is important is that just like Bavarians and Northern Germans have differences, in the United States and China, there are many regional differences. This means that generalizing and stereotyping can get us into trouble.

There are many dimensions to learn about but for your purposes, you need to tie them to the business environment, how you interact and how to communicate.

I will leave a series of documents for anyone interested to read and we can determine later if some training can help your company avoid some problems and costs caused by cultural differences.

Thank you very much and have a great day.

Certainly, many issues where miscommunication happened during the planning and set up of the facilities abroad came up.

The interesting thing was that there had been very little consideration for problems related to misunderstanding in the budgets and mostly the issues were solved as they came up without really thinking it was a general systematic problem that could create bigger problems.

Johannes and his team remained in the meeting room and reflected on a few other examples where each person had encountered an "intercultural" opportunity. One key learning that struck an important note for the team was Brigitte's description of low versus high context.

When the company operated in Germany and German was their main language, they were able to communicate the meaning of their ideas and instructions in a very effective way, often without having to repeat or clarify. The team found this synonymous with a low-context process where little was left to guessing or assumptions. Perhaps, there was a way to reach a similar level of efficiency and understanding when dealing with people in other countries?

Notes

1. Jim Womack, Mike Rother, and John Shook—Lean Enterprise Institute; SPi edition (June 1, 1999).
2. In German: good bye or cheers!
3. Geert Hofstede—Social Psychologist—https://www.geert-hofstede.com.
4. Edward T. Hall—Anthropologist—www.edwardthall.com.

Chapter 4

Standard Work for Global Teams

Johannes had taken notes on everything everyone from his team had contributed. At this time, he felt that the comments reflected also many of the things he had already heard from his staff in China and the United States, so he decided to use the information and attempt to drive more awareness. He knew this was just scratching the surface of very big topics and that at least with some added attention, people would find ways to avoid some of the waste.

He wrote in his notebook the crux of how he saw the situation:

> Now we have gone global and this means we have entered into a world of tremendous diversity. This diversity is represented in at least three items we have noticed: language, culture and distance and what we are experiencing is the impact of these on our timely coordination and to get things done effectively. More diversity creates opportunities for variance and where variance cannot be controlled or removed, we may experience more waste and more costs.
>
> Diversity is driving misunderstandings which then creates problems in our execution. If we can reduce some of the variance, maybe we can decrease some of the corresponding costs.
>
> If we can adopt some kind of standardization, like we did on our shop floor, to the way we interact with our people across the world, this should reduce some variance.

Standardize the WHO

Johannes needed a pause. He was somewhat overwhelmed by the amount of details he was now uncovering. He needed to reflect.

He realized that one of the things that was not working very well was the cross-functionality of his teams as they attempted to communicate across the oceans and time zones that separated them. One issue was that it was not absolutely clear to everyone who should be contacted for every topic in each location. This was in fact part of the variance some of his staff had told him was happening, which was causing wasted time.

Amazingly enough, this was happening even though the official organization charts were posted and available on the company's intranet.

Things were not in order.

In Germany, the labels used to name a specific job function were clear to everyone. Even across the industry, the names of the positions and the functions matched from company to company. So, it was taken for granted that this would be the same everywhere else. But soon the opposite was realized when the plants were established in China and the United States.

For example, a project team leader in Germany and a project manager in the United States might have similar labels but not necessarily be responsible for the same functions. And in China, the translated functions created a problem, adding to the already existing confusion created by local Chinese customs and hierarchies.

In earlier years, he had learned about 5S and participated in its first implementations at one of his plants. Johannes followed the topic for a few years, but was drawn away to deal with day-to-day problems. Nonetheless, something about 5S had stuck with him and he started to think if there was an angle to approach part of the current situation with this philosophy.

Specifically, he would use the second S to set things in order: everything in its place and a place for everything, he remembered and entered a quick note on his mobile phone: clearly defined roles and responsibilities.

Johannes knew they needed to set things in order around the chain of command. He had noticed a lot of time being wasted to waiting: for decisions, for finding whom to consult, or who was the right person to delegate to.

This would be the first standard that had to be created. It was clear that if people were to collaborate and interact effectively, they had to know, for example, who had what responsibility, who made decisions, and who was the next person in charge in case of escalations. In addition, many of the engineers had expectations tied to the title of the function. They expected a quality manager to solve all the quality problems of a specific area. The job title was being confused with the activities of the function which led to endless and wasteful arguments.

Johannes had noted and agreed with George Richards, the US manager, about the lack of cross-functionality.

He figured that once all functional roles were set in order and clearly defined throughout the world, this would help ensure adequate cross-functionality in the company and move away from some of the compartmentalized way of thinking in his company. He suspected that this way of thinking had contributed to the lack of order he was experiencing.

Johannes Boern *a place for everyone and everyone in their place*, and then called a meeting with his managers and explained what he was seeing and what he wanted to do.

STANDARD WORK IN THE COMMUNICATION PROCESS

Considering that every individual may tend to do things in a different way, a standard consists of an agreed upon series of steps to reach a specific goal, with the intention that everyone follows these steps the same way.

In addition, a standard can act as a type of rule that helps to set a preestablished target and in this sense, the preestablished target is also a standard.

In a manufacturing process, for example, an assembly operator must accurately follow a series of steps, for example, the standard process in order to reach an assembled product, for example, the preestablished target.

As things don't always go according to plan and stuff happens, having a standard creates a clear place to start the review of what went wrong, at which step in the process and what contributing factors may have had an effect on the deviation. In addition, it helps us observe clearly what we might want to update and change to the original standard so that the stuff that deviated can be avoided in the future.

People are the ones who agree to adhere to a standard way of doing something.

Unless a process is in place to establish absolute clarity about what steps to follow and what the expected outcomes are, people may follow different paths to get the work done. This means variance will be present.

How might we adopt such an important concept to improve the quality of our interactions?

Keep in mind that in this book, the discussion is about the communication that drives action along with an expectation of performance. This means that a specific goal is being sought after, as a result of coordinated actions.

To achieve its goals within the complexity in most organizations, it is essential to attain a series of well-coordinated actions between the different players in the different areas.

Agreements are the foundation of those coordinated actions.

The standard your organization relies on is in essence a series of agreements between all the stakeholders about what has to get done, who is going to do it, and by when.

Job Titles Might Not Mean the Same Thing

Johannes was having lunch with Klaus, a good friend and shared with him some of the issues Boern GMBH was encountering.

His friend interjected and told this story:

> I recall a situation that that created similar difficulties happened in Mexico. The European headquarters had assigned a Country Manager as the top level person in charge of the operation in that country. The Mexico plant was interdependent with the US facility and the direct customer contact was in the USA.
>
> Although the US plant had a CEO, the Country Manager in Mexico felt his position to be more important, after all his responsibility was related to the whole country and therefore the US CEO was below him. Headquarters behaved very ambiguously in these matters and did not clarify the matter on the global organization chart which in turn exacerbated a problem fired by the egos of the two players.
>
> One additional title that they had in Mexico is that of the Director General. A title I have not yet seen in US companies. While it also sounds like a very top level function, it has to fit the context of the type of business and the actual responsibility and authority the person in this function has.
>
> In another case, the Director General was in charge of ensuring that the materials and equipment provided by the US mother plant were effectively taken care of. In addition, his task was to maintain an excellent relationship with the local operators and administrative team and with the local government.
>
> However, in both cases, decisions were being made locally in Mexico, without consulting or agreeing with the US plant. At the end, the decisions impacted the performance of the company, to

the point the customer was affected and the issue got escalated until the functions were finally clarified and standardized.

Klaus ended his story by recommending to Johannes that instead of taking a job title at face value, a clarifying conversation should take place to determine what each player actually does, what are his or her activities and responsibilities. The clarity required is about the activities, not the label given to th person.

Johannes thanked Klaus for the examples and shared with him his thoughts about the use of Lean to improves such sitations as Klasu had brought up.

SMALL AND MEDIUM SIZED BUSINESS

It's quite possible that in larger corporations this is a topic that is taken into consideration as the organization charts are drawn and as part of a normal corporate initiative. Even in large corporations though, I've seen otherwise.

There are thousands more small- and medium-sized business than there are large corporations and these smaller and sometimes less sophisticated enterprises grow in a way that is not necessarily planned out in a deliberate and structured way. Many go through organic growth and adapt to their new size in a less than organized way.

This might mean that roles and responsibilities can become a hodgepodge of functions sometimes with a less than clear way how each interacts with another and nonstandard titles or labels are given to people's roles.

It's normal to encounter in smaller, family-owned businesses hybrid roles or roles with paternalistic sounding labels.

Because so many small- and medium-sized businesses support larger corporations as suppliers and service providers the interactions between the two require a clear understanding of the actual meaning of someone's title in order to determine who will actually interface with them.

Setting in Order: Everyone in Their Place and a Place for Everyone

The most typical way to depict an organization is by using a vertical chart (Figure 4.1) which gives us the illusion that value is being added as people work with their reports and their bosses. However, we know that in reality, there is a horizontal and diagonal interaction (Figure 4.2) required to

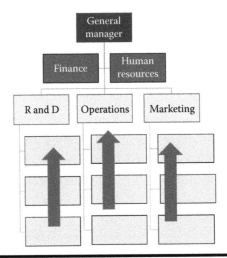

Figure 4.1   This is how some of us think value flows.

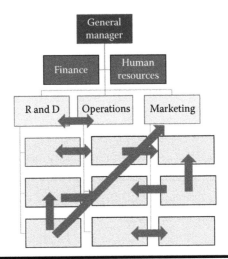

Figure 4.2   This is how value flows and how your customer perceives it.

produce and deliver a product or a service to the customer. It is the quality of these horizontal and diagonal interactions that will add value to your customer. In any case, in a global setting (Figure 4.3), there is no choice but to interact horizontally; otherwise, products will not be made, not be made on time, or might be made incorrectly.

This is not a new discussion and many organizations still represent their chain of command in a vertical, pyramid-shaped chart that starts at the top with a CEO and flows from top to bottom with functional areas and support staff until it ends with the bottom of the pyramid representing the front lines

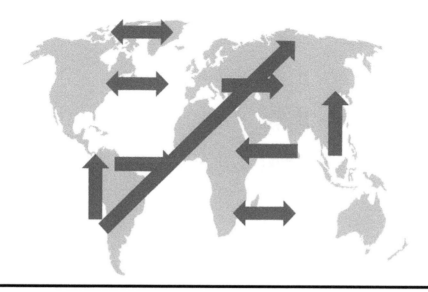

Figure 4.3   In our new gemba, this is how value flows.

of workers and operators. It is not very clear with this type of chart, how people from different areas actually interact—or should interact—to create the value required to satisfy a customer (Figures 4.1 through 4.3).

If we consider that the strategic plans of a company are accomplished by completing various programs that in turn are made up of a series of many small and large projects, we could enhance and complement our organization charts by using the RACI methodology many project teams have adopted.

Although projects imply an activity that is limited to a specific time and reaching a specific goal, we can observe how most organizations function via a series of small projects happening every day where people have to accomplish daily tasks. Any series of tasks might be looked at as a project.

In any case, one thing we learn from successful project teams is to have clearly defined, and accepted, roles and responsibilities for each of its members. Many teams use RACI as the basis for accomplishing this clarity and is an effective way to create a standard.

RACI[1] is an acronym that stands for responsible, accountable, consulted, and informed. This is a great methodology that clearly expresses who is responsible for what, the ultimately accountable person, and those that need to participate with information or be informed about what is happening (Figure 4.4).

Although it is quite possible that once some type of RACI methodology is implemented to clarify the current chain of command, it makes sense to

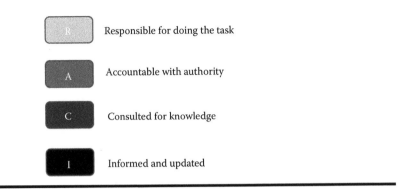

Figure 4.4   A basic description of the RACI acronym.

continually review the chart and not rely solely on how the current teams are set. Owing to turnover and growth, people leave and new people come in to organizations.

Evidently, five S and visual management are great partners in driving clarity into seemingly complicated situations. In the case of Boern GMBH, they adopted the methodology and working together with each plant they accurately identified the corresponding job functions and matched them to a RACI style matrix which was subsequently posted for everyone to see and keep updated. Project managers were made ultimately responsible to maintain them in conjunction with Boern's human resources team.

One Common Language

Johannes himself was an engineer and had become very self-aware of some of the constraints and deficiencies his training had given him. While he and his fellow engineers had excellent technical skills to address product and process problems, the new type of situations his company was encountering required different skills.

Most of the current issues were associated with inadequate interactions between the different global team players. This meant that the skills required were tied to the ability to function in an intercultural setting and achieve clarity when communicating with people from different countries.

And as an organization, a large percentage of Boern's staff were engineers who were typically not very good with these skills and had little to no training.

This realization identified a gap between what once functioned well and what was required now in the new, international Boern GMBH.

As an initial step, Johannes decided he would establish two key initiatives in his company:

1. English technical proficiency
2. Intercultural awareness

He made some notes and crafted the following message to Katharina, his HR team leader:

> Dear Katharina,
>
> As part of our journey to expand our organization outside of the borders of Germany we have encountered some problems and issues that have impacted our operations.
>
> Some of these problems are associated with the less than excellent way in which our employees interact which creates a lot of waste and unnecessary costs.
>
> For this reason, I ask that you prepare a proposal for me and our management team to enhance the skill of our staff in English and Intercultural knowledge.
>
> What I see is that while many of our team members have a basic knowledge of the English language, the business language with specific terms and vocabulary of our organization and automotive environment require people to acquire specific skills in this sense.
>
> So, we are looking for a way to learn the specific English of our industry and attain technical proficiency in this language.
>
> In addition, it seems we have been trying to manage our foreign plants from a German point of view and this is causing problems with our international partners. So, we have to learn about our own culture and the culture of others, like we saw in the brief presentation we had last month.
>
> Please contact me with any questions and I look forward to your proposal expecting a first draft by end of next week.
>
> Thanks
> Johannes Boern
> CEO

THE MOST BASIC STANDARD

A common language is definitely a great standard to establish when we have to interact with people from different countries. Not having such an agreement could derail practically any strategy. Once an agreement is reached on what the common language is, technical proficiency should be a goal to strive for every person that interacts in the global supply chain.

Nevertheless, knowing more than one language is also as important if your role requires communicating with global players. Some things cannot be said in a particular language, for example, and the relationship one can gain by speaking someone else's language cannot be emphasized enough.

The Impact of Nonstandard Work

Boern GMBH had recently ordered a critical piece of equipment needed in the US facility from an OEM in Spain. The machine was a key device that was needed to produce critical components for the Zenssor211 for North American clients. The lead time had been stipulated in the contract as 20 weeks. This machine supplier had an excellent track record with their quality and delivery in Europe.

As they were getting close to the delivery deadline, the traffic and logistics area requested the status and readiness of the equipment so that we could better ensure a match to the project plan, installation, and training.

Until then, there had been no updates from the supplier.

The reply from the supplier was that the equipment fabrication and testing would be delayed by about 10 days due to the lack of availability of some subsystem device from an outsourced supplier in France. However, insofar as the delivery of the machine to the United States, the OEM informed Boern that they could still match the quoted lead time. Something was not adding up and in the emails, it became apparent that the OEM had been referring to the delivery date to the port in Spain—not the total lead time needed for it to reach the facility across the Atlantic.

Compared with the original project timeline, the order arrived in the US plant 3 weeks late. This caused a longer lead time to install the machine and train the operators. In addition, the machine was a crucial piece of equipment needed to test the characteristics of molded resin and this was a huge impact on the development of prototypes bound for the Zenssor211.

For one, a misunderstood logistic term contributed to the delay. The fact that there was no agreement with the supplier to notify Boern's logistics of any delay was also a factor, and not having weekly acknowledgments that things were going according to plan made things even worse.

Of course, there was the obvious finger pointing process, full of opinions and different perspectives from each participant. However, there was no standard agreement and therefore each person saw things differently.

The Agreement Model: A Standard for Action

Interactions and transactions such as the one Boern experienced are constantly taking place in a business environment. When people from different countries are interacting and trying to get things done quickly, many assumptions and individual interpretations are made. There never seems to be enough time to verify if everyone is on the same page and everyone assumes things were clear to every stakeholder.

My experience has shown me otherwise and the time spent on ensuring everyone understands what they have to do, in order for a successful result to take place, is time well spent.

There is a continuous series of agreements that have to happen in any organization in order for things to get done—as close to a plan as possible.

Agreements such as the ones that attorneys prepare are intended to cover as many aspects as possible to ensure every party involved has the same understanding on the matter at hand.

At the very least, an agreement should cover who is going to do what by when.

However, if we are aware of Murphy's law and the existence of entropy,[2] then it makes sense to prepare for when things don't go according to plan. This is where spelling out ahead of time any possible contingencies makes good sense. The key here is to agree on what actions should be taken, and by whom should things deviate from their original plan.

Finally, any agreement will be greatly enhanced if the dates, times, and places of all follow-up activities are stated and understood by everyone.

In the circumstances Boern GMBH is navigating, it can be of great help to design and determine a way everyone can be on the same page. This will certainly help reduce the variance and avoid costly misunderstandings.

The model outlined below can help guide anyone in establishing a standard by which one or more persons will interact.

You will notice the question WHY also makes up part of the model. The reason is that with the use of this question, everyone can be made aware of the relevance and importance of the activity that needs to take place—engaging the people to interact in a positive way.

The Model

Who: Who is the team leader? What does his or her role mean? Who is responsible to execute? Who has the knowledge? Needs to be consulted? Who participates in a decision?

What: What has to get done? What are the activities? What is the target? What information, resources, equipment are required? What is the expected outcome?

When: When to start? Dates of milestones? End date?

Where: Where do we meet? Physical location and virtual meeting information. Where does an action or delivery take place? Complete address info.

Why: Why is the activity important? What are some potential consequences if the goal is not met? How does this tie into the customer?

What if: Agree on what to do when things don't go according to plan. Note: the longer the time and wider the distance, the more the need to agree on what-ifs.

What's next: How often do we meet? Where? At what time? Who needs to be there? Note: use the reminder meetings to reset the targets, the agreements and remind everyone about the "why."

Applying the Model

Here is an example of how an agreement using this model could have been established on a project such as the equipment ordered from the OEM in Spain.

Ed Harris, Boern's customer logistics manager, reviews the contract and the supplier's quote and sends out the following email to Julia, the supplier's sales representative:

Hello Julia,

I wanted to make sure we have all the facts correctly. The equipment will be delivered by you on March 15, 2003. The terms of delivery mean that you are already including in your lead time the days it takes for ocean freight across the Atlantic to the Port of

Charleston, South Carolina. So we understand that the equipment will arrive at the Port of Charleston on or before March 15. If this is not accurate, please correct our assumption.

In addition, in case anything does not go according to plan, we would like to be notified immediately so that we can work together to ensure our project does not suffer any delay. The equipment is crucial to one of our main projects and the deadline is dependent on the timely delivery of your machine. Our customers would be very upset if we can't deliver their products on time.

Can you also confirm that we can establish a quick telephone call every Thursday morning at 10 a.m. your time, to confirm with you the status of the build of our equipment?

Please respond back with any suggestions from your side that can help this project meet its deadline.

Feel free to call me on my mobile phone 24/7 with any questions or concerns.

Sincerely,
Ed Harris
Logistics Manager.…..

Had this been done at the onset of the project, Ed's team would have an excellent position to request coverage for any unbudgeted costs.

This email example covers all of the points outlined in the agreement model. In a situation where language, culture, and distance can affect a transaction or a project in a negative way, we suggest a model such as this one which could serve to establish the standard work required to achieve a specific goal.

If we refer back to high- and low-context cultures, following a process such as this agreement model ensures that every base is covered. It reflects a very low-context process intended to drive absolute clarity and reduce any ambiguity.

Take a look at the following example of standard work agreements in action from a real situation:

Harry: Good morning Marcel, I wanted to take the opportunity to celebrate the end of your 90-day training period. Congratulations! (Marcel Thanks Harry).

From what I've seen and heard you are ready to take on the responsibility as Operations Manager for plant 3. We have provided all the resources you need. Can we agree that as part of your new role, you will ensure a productivity gain of 0.6% every quarter? And that it will be measured based on our SAP Pro system.

Marcel: Yes Harry, in principle I can agree for the first 3 quarters of the year. However, I would like to ask you to consider a slightly reduced gain for the last quarter—say 0.55—as you know, Christmas season is challenging for the workers. At the Harry time, I would look for ways to compensate the other quarters with a slightly better gain.

Harry: So if I hear you correctly, you are asking to modify the goals based on seasonality. I think it makes sense and I can change the targets for your area to match this. Is there anything else you may want to add to the agreement?

Marcel: Actually yes Harry, I would like to have IT provide the productivity information every week. Then I can review and make sure it is taking into account all the information.

Harry: Sure, I think that makes good sense and is very fair. Is there something else you can think of?

Marcel: No Harry. I thank you for your flexibility and hearing me out. I'm ready to take on the challenge.

Harry: Well, I do have a couple of more points we have to agree on. First of all, I believe in Murphy's law which causes things to not go according to plan. So I would like your agreement that you let me know way ahead of time if the productivity gain is not going to be met. I also have to report to my boss and to the board. In fact, at any given time if you notice anything that can impact this goal—please let me know immediately. Then we can meet again and if needed and together agree on something different.

Marcel: Of course that makes a lot of sense. I can agree to this.

Harry: One last thing Marcel, we meet every other Monday in conference room # 3 at 9 a.m. to report out to the other managers the status of our area. This is yet another forum to bring up any variances to our plan. I want to make sure you will be there for those meetings.

Marcel: Yes I will be there.

Harry: (shaking hands) It's great to have you on board!

Note that in this situation Marcel does not have to accept the terms of the agreement right away or as they are presented. Marcel could choose to say

Yes, I agree or No, I don't agree and will not commit. In addition, he might promise to review the issue and commit to get back with a reply within 24 hours or a counter offer.

The process of agreeing on a standard could follow one of these four paths:

1. Yes—complete agreement and commitment
2. No—no agreement
3. Agree-to-commit—a promise to get back with a response at a specific time
4. A counter offer—agreeing but proposing some specific changes

Marcel provided a counter offer and in this case, Harry considered it made sense and accepted it. Harry could have stuck to his original proposal as well and perhaps Marcel would have not committed or requested to get back with Harry at a later date.

Now, we have a standard agreement that can be used to make sure that Marcel follows his process to achieve his goals.

What to do when things don't go according to plan?

In a manufacturing process, when a bad part is produced or when the agreed upon efficiency is not being reached, we can use the standard process to go back and review in each step, what may have been done different than the agreed upon way.

In a commitment agreement, we can actually do the same since we have actually covered in detail the who, what, when, etc.

Here are Harry and Marcel meeting again, after the expected results did not pan out:

Marcel: You wanted to see me Harry?

Harry: Well Marcel, the productivity figures for last quarter were way below what was expected. We agreed to 0.6% and the figure is at 0.47% the report has already gone out and now my boss is going to be asking questions.

Marcel: Yes, actually the reason is that the sales department booked a lot of low-volume sales and this impacted our line scheduling. They did not consider how this was going to affect the productivity of the plant.

Harry: So, I understand that because of sales your productivity went below what we agreed to?

Marcel: Yes and I was too preoccupied with keeping the process running smoothly so that all the orders could be fulfilled. So, it was tough to let you know about the hit to productivity ahead of time.

Harry: And so you were preoccupied with the production and therefore did not call me even though you agreed to let me know if something could affect the productivity.

Marcel: Well, there was nothing I could do. Maybe we need to call sales to discuss the issue?

Harry: Marcel, you and I agreed to the 0.6% and now we are way below. In addition, you did not let me know ahead of time and now the report is out to our board.

Marcel: Well, some of the workers were not trained for changing over quickly to support smaller orders, so there was a lot of time lost to waiting.

Harry: If I hear you correctly, the operators could not respond properly to the type of orders. Marcel, you and I had an agreement and I expected 0.6% productivity, not it's at 0.47%.

Marcel: Yes, in fact there was a lot of people absent. Maybe we should call the HR department and they can explain.

Harry: I understand your idea of the HR department, however, I expected the % number we agreed to and that you would let me know ahead of time.

Marcel: OK. Harry, look I messed up and I apologize. Here's what I can do. I will review the sales plan again and establish a plan to recover some of the lost productivity. I will make sure to train the operators for a similar situation in the future and will also make sure to let you know immediately when I see productivity being hit this way. Then maybe we can work with the team and figure out a way to avoid this in the future.

Harry: I accept your plan. Let's meet next week and check in on how you are executing on this.

If you notice, Harry has a clear advantage in this interaction—not because he might be the manager—but because there is a standard agreement which he can and does revert back at all times. There are no opinions or viewpoints to discuss here. No need to get excited or emotional. Simply put in black and white: Marcel was to follow the standard, but he did not.

In fact, an equally important part of the agreement was not respected by Marcel: the what if.

Harry was open to the possibility of things not going according to plan. This is a reality in business and while we cannot have absolute control over what actually happens—we are still responsible to manage each situation as it arises. Considering the complexity associated with global supply chains and virtual teams, the topic of contingencies requires ample attention.

Agreeing on the course of action when a contingency arises is as important as the complete agreement. Aside from man-made situations that may have an impact on the plan and the original outcome—sometimes Mother Nature plays a role in disrupting standard agreements.

While a volcano, earthquake, or tsunami may create some disorder and impact an agreement, it will still be up to people to meet and reach new agreements on how to interact to keep the situation moving forward.

Notes

1. For more info on RACI visit: http://www.racitraining.com/.
2. Lack of order or predictability; gradual decline into disorder.

Chapter 5

PDCA: Learning by Trying

What is the Meaning of Your Communication?

Johannes Boern had already realized that he had a high degree of fault in what was happening in his company. It dawned on him that a key part of the PDCA (plan–do–check–act) process his company had implemented was limited to their technical and production areas. Because most of their focus was on the production process side and little on the processes associated with getting things done outside of manufacturing, he and his management team based their activities, decisions, and execution on partial and incomplete information, when the new, uncharted chapter of expanding to another country came up at Boern GMBH.

There is no cookie-cutter formula for success—and certainly not one when going global. However, adopting a scientific method such as PDCA in your activities may afford a better path and help avoid some costly mistakes.[1] In our intercultural training, for example, my team insists that every participant avoid a standard book definition for the culture they interact with. The reason is that there are individual differences, based on each person's unique education and upbringing. In addition, the fact that cultures are experiencing constant change is pointed out, as the Internet of things, globalization and immigration, are tangible factors that are driving transformation in every society.

Since it is impossible to know how each person is programmed, one can explore by preempting a conversation with someone from another culture by stating upfront how you are new at this, that you want to learn about them, and that you have no intention to disrespect or insult. At the very least, you have expressed your basic human concerns which typically should also match those of the person(s) you are attempting to establish a working relationship with. In almost every case, before a transaction occurs, the first step is to establish a relationship, without which no trust will have been created. Without trust, the rest of your interaction will largely be flawed.

Crafting a Message to be Understood

The response that you get is the meaning of your communication.[2]

Stated in our context: the results triggered by your communication will expose what was understood by the other person. This expression also offers a perspective we can adopt in our case to drive Improvements in the effectiveness of our interactions, through better communication.

For example, if you adopt PDCA thinking, you can use it as a first step in establishing the relationship by adjusting your message based on the reactions you get from the people you are interacting with. Once you have established the relationship, you can start your conversation for action, all the time checking how the meaning is received and adjusting accordingly. This is a learning loop, which means the next time you interact, there's a much better chance the meaning of your message is better understood by the other person.

In a few of the examples of the situations Boern experienced, the results were definitely not the expected ones and accounted for numerous delays to projects, productivity losses, and human talent opportunity costs. There were misunderstandings, under-communication, and the meanings conveyed were not understood the same way by the receiving parties. In a nutshell, poor results reflected the mismatched meanings of their messages.

The use of PDCA may sound similar to what communication experts refer to reflective listening. However, in the case of global execution one must keep in mind that many interactions happen in virtual environments. Emails, phone calls, and teleconferences have become ways to interact that unfortunately do not allow for immediate feedback to be received from participants. When we are face to face with people, we can glean whether a person has understood our message through nonverbal cues. Not so in a virtual environment, thus making it quite a challenge to determine if the meaning of your message was accurately understood.

A PDCA mindset will help drive a true understanding, and create a better chance to improve the intended execution.

After some of the costly errors, this was now much clearer to many at Boern and especially to Johannes who as a leader made sure everyone on the team realized that the processes of communication were as important as any other process. Knowing that there was a need to improve how meanings were conveyed, he requested that his subordinates consider a few changes in the way they should interact.

First, he requested that everyone take responsibility for delivering their messages in a clear, unambiguous, and complete way. This meant becoming aware of the speed, the accent, and avoiding the use of fancy words that add no value and are prone to create confusion.

Johannes also recommended not blurting out 10 ideas at a time, and instead just one at a time as this would allow to establish how a specific message was received, avoiding the effect of people naturally blocking out messages as protection for information overloads. In addition, ensuring that the complete idea and all the information were provided would also be an important change.

Second, he asked that everyone asks what the other person understood in their own words. This allowed participants to make sure the meaning was being transferred adequately.

And third, Johannes set the expectation for everyone to learn from each Transaction: what worked and what hindered the process of creating a full understanding, free from any ambiguity (Figures 5.1).

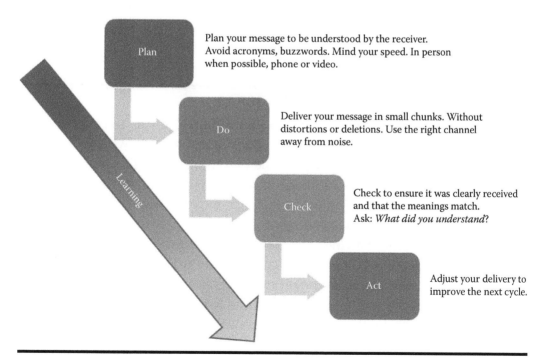

Figure 5.1 Consider using this model with someone you are just meeting or someone you have experienced problems understanding, and being understood.

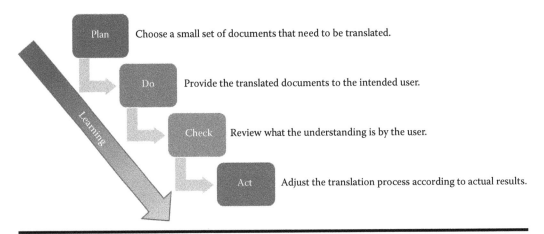

Figure 5.2   An example for using PDCA instead of batch processing for translations.

The use of PDCA in other communication processes is further explored on Figure 5.2. In the case of imprecise, batch translations that contributed to even poorer and costlier results in lost time and talent.

On a final note, going to the gemba is a proven way to perform the check portion of PDCA. Considering the distance factor in our new gemba when things have to get done with the participation of international supply chain partners, get creative and adopt PDCA to make sure you are able to see and learn, from how others understood your message.

PLAN YOUR MESSAGE TO BE UNDERSTOOD

If we decide to take responsibility to send a message that will be understood by our receiver, perhaps the first thing to do is to assume that we are the supplier and our receiver is our customer. Then by using a scientific trial-and-error approach, such as PDCA we can begin to realize what we may be contributing when things don't get done properly. Once we are aware of this, we can make certain adjustments to ensure our message is clearly understood. Let's use the example of the drawings that were being used to transfer the low volume product lines to Boern's US plant. The plan was to translate the entire set of drawings and specs of all the products that were on the list to be transferred. The hypothesis may have been that the translations provided would be understood 100% by the American team. The process of translation was performed in a batch approach and the control of the effectiveness was not done by anyone in the United States and instead was reviewed by engineers in Germany through a random sampling. It is important to note that a process of trial and error will be much more productive when performed in small, incremental steps.

Once a result is in, we can review it, check against the intended outcome, and adjust and make another small change to our hypothesis and the experiment itself. This process of small experiments will tend to yield a lot of lessons learned and avoids making huge investments based on beautifully justified paper projects. Identifying problems while they are small is a much better situation than not seeing the problems, letting them fester, and grow into complex and costly state. While Johannes Boern and his engineers were following a similar, scientific approach to design and improve continually their speed sensors, they did not realize that other types of processes exist that are crucial to tie one part of the company to the other and that a similar continuous improvement methodology could have been used in the case of the drawings. A better way to execute the project might have been to select five or ten products randomly or with a certain classification of their complexity. Have the corresponding drawings and specs translated and subsequently reviewed by their customer, in this case, their own American engineers.

In all probability, the feedback would have triggered an alarm to have a closer look at the translations, the handwritten notes, and the specific design details that were not represented clearly in print.

Notes

1. For a history of the PDCA/PDSA cycle visit: https://www.deming.org/sites/default/files/pdf/2015/PDSA_History_Ron_Moen.pdf.
2. Richard Bandler. *Frogs into Princes: Neuro Linguistic Programming*, Real People Press, 1979.

Chapter 6

Lessons from Boern in the New Gemba

Kami and Johannes were finally able to meet personally for a few hours when their trips coincided in the United States. Even their ability to meet face to face suffered the same types of causes that Boern GMBH had been experiencing the past years—their physical separation influenced the availability of Kami to be present to help uncover and solve the matters at hand.

Kami was presenting at a local conference and agreed to meet Johannes early in the morning at his hotel lobby. He greeted Johannes and after some small talk they got down to business.

Kami: In a sense Johannes, the issue is not different than the past. In order to get things done your engineers had to interact with each other and also with purchasing, logistics, controlling, and other areas. But the execution then happened in a timely manner because most of the players were there, close by and also you spoke the same language. Because you saw this quite seamless, you paid the most attention to technical issues and production issues.

OK. So let's take a look at the bigger picture and try to figure out what things you can do to reduce the negative impact of today's situation, because I assume you will open plants in other countries later, right? And remember, you still have several new products in development and to set up the plant in China—so these must be protected from such issues.

Johannes: Absolutely, the past is past. It wasn't easy then, but now I realize that we also had interdependence then but with certain advantages that blinded us to the true complexity.

Here is what I think, and please tell me how you see it.

We are used to making very detailed plans and we gather a lot of input before we determine the plans are ready to launch a project. We did it like in the past with a lot of technical knowledge and technical experience. When we have such level of detail we always had success in the past.

In reality, relying so much on competencies that helped us in the past, also blinded us to the fact that those same competencies were not enough in today's environment and circumstances.

Kami: Yes, yes Johannes, no experimentation. No PDCA. Just planning is very typical of many companies and this gets them into trouble. But of course, in order to check, and verify with certainty what is really happening with respect to the plan, you must go to the gemba, and now it is not always possible to do so when it's outside your four walls. Sorry to interrupt, please continue.

Johannes: Also, we were quite naïve in thinking that we could copy paste our processes in other plants. So we were assuming that everyone thinks and acts the same way as we do. I'm saying this and I feel stupid because intellectually I obviously know this is not true. But maybe we wanted to believe it and justify our budgets and project plans. Everything looks so good on paper.

I think the biggest factor that affected our Zenssor211 project was the distance between us and the other plants where we were coordinating sample and prototype trials with tooling and materials. The teleconferences were often messy, our guys could not understand our foreign colleagues, and vice versa. And the lead times to get samples back and forth increased dramatically, compared with how it was when we did it all locally.

Also, we provided the same drawings and work instructions we had always used in Germany to our plants in China and the United States, thinking that they would understand things the same way we did. And of course our documents were not perfect, because we relied on the proximity of our teams to very quickly and personally clarify any doubts.

And of course, since we are so technology driven, we assumed that buying some fancy ERP software would make us more efficient and solve all our problems. Maybe we could have done a better job at implementing the software and the interfaces but even so, I still see the need to have people on the front lines taking care of things. Technology will not replace them. People will ultimately be needed to take care of and solve the variance to the plans.

Kami: My dear Johannes, I would like to point out that the underlying issue as you say is unclear communication that leads to misunderstandings. So this is a topic that you and your teams have to become very aware of.

But the main problem this miscommunication presents is the loss of time.

As we discussed zero-based thinking means that every activity has to be scrutinized. And we also said that every coordinated activity is preceded by some type of order, request, or decision, all of which have to in some form or other be communicated. When things are not clear, then the people must interpret, explain, repeat, wait, etc., and these are activities that do not add any value, from the customer's perspective.

Johannes: Kami, you know this usually did not happen when we were just doing business in Germany. Our language is very precise and everyone understood clearly and exactly what action needed to be done, so coordination was not the focus of our problems.

Kami: Absolutely true. This is now different, isn't it? Here is a bigger problem though Johannes, you don't have unlimited resources. In fact, you thought that the investment in technology would free up some of your teams' time to take care of Zenssor211. Instead of having some key people available in your development process, they were sucked into the day to day needs to keep the plants running in order to satisfy the immediate requirements of your customers.

When resources are limited, time cannot be wasted on anything and I think you have seen your share of waste you did not see before.

Johannes: Thank you for pointing this out Kami. To talk about communication is a big topic, but knowing how it affects our operation is key. Time is certainly a factor we have always paid attention to, like: make more in less time. Because we took for granted that we could continue to execute in an efficient manner, we did not look at the loss of time to other activities and how this would impact our resources.

I trust my closest engineers and am sure of what they are capable of doing. But they cannot be in three places at the same time and take care of every issue. So there is the issue of priorities and the availability of the same people to take care of problems. Again, trying to stick to a budget, we decided we did not need to hire or train personnel in key roles. I had the "old ways" hat on and I thought the same people could lead the projects in the United States and China effectively.

Kami: Absolutely Johannes. Do you remember the meaning of muri? It is about overburdening your resources and processes. People get overwhelmed and then they are prone to making mistakes. Those mistakes can then create muda because you have to correct things and because other people are waiting. The stories you told me reflect this.

But again, the biggest problem is time, because there is no time invested to reflect, to think what is happening, and try to improve. People stay busy firefighting and leave no time for making improvements. This is a bad situation for any company to be in.

Then we should revisit one of the less discussed inner workings of Toyota, which is to clearly define how people connect. Remember that you cannot pass electric current when the wires are not connected. Same thing happens, as you have experienced, when people are not connected. This is where a common language like English has to be defined. It is the standard to communicate with most of the world. Similar to the standard you discussed before where everyone spoke German and communicated in a clear and precise way. Then your project teams and functional teams should receive a deep training in intercultural behaviors. Not only from a book, but live action learning so that the people can feel how and why other people think the way they do. These things cannot be underestimated.

I think Johannes that if your company confronted the very complex issues brought by globalization the same way you dealt with complex technical issues, you would be very successful.

Johannes: Perhaps you are right Kami. One thing for us is that we were so focused on technical skills and the use of technology but the basic building block that is required for people to communicate to do their job. The proof is in where we spend money in our budget: a lot on technology and zero on language skills.

WHAT CAUSED THE DELAYS OF ZENSSOR211?

For the participants in the sessions, the exercise at first was difficult, especially the engineers who were trained to use this type of methodology to solve product and process quality issues. Nonetheless, the diagram they were able to pull together provides a good set of issues the team considered important. They identified the fact that technical English proficiency was lacking at many levels and this factor alone triggered many other problems. Lack of intercultural awareness was also pointed out, with large emphasis on the differences between the way things are communicated and done in Germany, versus how the employees at the plant in China behave. This created misunderstandings that drove a lot of waiting and delays in getting things done. In addition, the time zone factor was mentioned as a factor that contributed to multiple interruptions and intervals of time where no value was being added. Besides the fact that often it was difficult to schedule meetings where everyone required could be present, the distance also affected the delivery times of important prototypes and samples that needed to be measured and reviewed by all the teams. Perhaps a key negative component of the different time zones was the fact that people communicated too much via email with little personal contact by phone or face to face. Knowledge transfer was also a factor that repeatedly came up. Nevertheless, a systemic root cause analysis was needed in order to prevent as much as possible some of these issues from recurring. The closest the team came to mentioning a possible systemic issue is the cookie-cutter approach added to the corporate culture bone, where the discussion pointed to the factors that had made Boern successful in the past and drove a cookie-cutter approach to the company's expansion into a global setting (Figure 6.1).

Kami: I need a moment. Kami put up his palm and fell into a deep silence. After a few moments he sat upright and provided the following advice to Johannes.

I have to get going in the next hour but I want to provide you with the following thoughts. What Boern GMBH is living is very tied to a structural situation and we have to be very aware of it and understand it so we can determine courses of action.

What I mean is the structure of your company and also the industry you are in. It is a very competitive environment and getting more and more because new players are entering from countries that did not compete before. Sure you can pretend you are the best, but you already saw how another company took over the

Factors that influenced execution and the delay of zenssor211

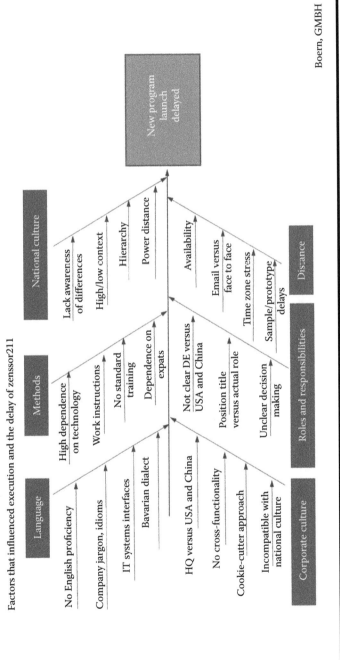

Boern, GMBH

Figure 6.1 This fishbone diagram is from one of the Boern meetings where the team tried to establish the main contributing root causes that impacted the execution of the Zenssor211 program.

opportunity of the Zenssor211. Not because the technology and idea were bad, but because the speed of execution was too slow.

So I think the structure you have carried until today, based on how your grandfather set things up is meeting up with the realities of a new environment. You are set up in a traditional vertical way, and a standard way exists: who reports to whom. etc.… But your departments must work together in a horizontal way, and no standard for this is defined. In fact, you don't have anyone except yourself, that brings every area together to connect with each other properly.

Johannes: Even my budget is set up this way.

Kami: Many people in the Lean community are talking about assigning managers to value streams which means going across departments and functions to see the complete process and where value is being added.

And this is a good way to look at your situation but we must also consider the bigger picture, where you have to interact with players from other organizations, sometimes in other countries in order to completely fulfill your customer's expectations: quality, delivery, and cost.

So we mentioned interdependence earlier because this is reality. We cannot do things by ourselves. Then the question is, what do we have to do to make sure the interactions needed between all the players run as smooth as possible. Just like the continuous, uninterrupted flow that you want to attain in your production processes. Do you follow?

Johannes: Yes, I do. This is quite eye opening for me. I am so used to our structure it has actually blinded us from seeing things from a different perspective.

Kami: Well then Johannes, I think you can get your team to map out the top level value streams between departments and across the oceans and do it with everyone in the room. This way each person will see how their work influences the process.

Johannes: This will take some time to do, and on the surface it seems like spending time not on our core business, but I can see where it will be a good investment because we will actually see where we can reduce wasted time from our out of control communication processes.

Kami: I was afraid you would fall into the "time is money" mindset because many executives will consider such an exercise as a waste. One advantage is that you can deliberately control and plan to spend the time to study how the connections are happening today and what you may have to do to standardize how people must connect to get the job done.

I know from the companies that I am working with now and that are quite successful even in this new globalized supply chain that the key factors they realized were essential had less to do with technology and more with people. In one of the companies, an executive summarized it like this: "In this new gemba, we must have very focused teams that are perfectly aligned to produce rapid response to changing customer demand." I agree with him and also might add that the teams have to be friendly, which can mean they have intercultural awareness, which is a topic you also mentioned earlier.

One last thought that I think is quite important for you and your Lean culture. If the world is changing, then the way we approach Lean might also need to change along with it.

Johannes was taking notes and his mind was racing with ideas on how he would kick off the new Boern GMBH to meet and match the challenges of the new gemba.

Johannes: Kami, as always your observations are extremely helpful. I certainly have a lot of work to do on my side to get things started. Once I'm ready, I would like you to join us and participate in the transformation. Please check your calendar and let me know when you will be available so we can book your visits to our plants.

Kami: Very glad to be of help and I wish you good luck. I will send you my available dates very soon.

They shook hands and parted until the next time.

Conclusion

As leaders, we can certainly decide to pick and choose what waste streams we will take care of to remain competitive. Chances are though, that other companies will beat you to the punch and realize that when every second counts, every type of waste must be unearthed and dealt with, which consequently might result in a competitive edge, for them.

Our hero in the story, Boern GMBH is starting a new facet of his Lean journey for the reason that previously unknown, unplanned challenges and obstacles inadvertently crept into his business. This is a common theme with many of the companies I've worked with, and which I find is still not being paid sufficient attention to. And this is not difficult to understand, considering humans run companies and as humans we tend to focus on physical things. We tend not to notice other "invisible" factors that affect our results. Additionally, many of us are commonly educated to take care of material problems while we receive little education on finding real solutions for the invisible, "soft" issues.

The current state of trade in the world demands a new approach, taking into account the unprecedented degree of interdependence we have created in our supply chains. This global trend is also introducing new competitors from countries that we once only sold to. Nonetheless, in this new gemba, your customer expects to be served with excellent quality, on time delivery at an acceptable cost; so we must get rid of any complacency and learn to see any and all hidden forces that could be contributing toward waste and unwanted costs.

Undoubtedly, technology is great at supporting the way we connect and at providing the information available to make decisions. Nonetheless, we will continue to depend on the people on the front lines to take care of the countless unexpected things that will not go according to plan, greatly impacted by the accelerated speed of innovation and seemingly reckless changes in customer tastes.

The success—or failure—of a task, a project, or a program depends on the quality of the connections and interactions these people have, which demands perfectly clear and unambiguous communication. Understanding that communication precedes activities, we might save precious seconds and minutes in physical processes if we can get our message across unambiguously right the first time.

I often see companies successfully bringing about solutions to highly complex problems. Often this takes an exceedingly specialized creative problem-solving mindset, and a lot of effort. If a company were to utilize this same mindset to approach the subject of communication, recognizing it as the complex problem it truly is, perhaps some nice surprises would emanate from such efforts. Things like innovation, productivity, and profitability might mysteriously improve by having taken care of some previously invisible factors. I'm convinced this is where your competitive advantage lies.

Finally, like any other philosophy, Lean is continuously evolving. And this is a good thing considering that the world is also changing and transforming the context and circumstances where business is happening. It certainly makes little sense to keep our blinders on and go about our daily jobs without acknowledging and addressing issues that have a hard impact on our bottom lines. Therefore, our Lean journey will be greatly enhanced if we adopt Lean communication as a complement to an already powerful and successful management philosophy.

How about you? How will you adapt your Lean thinking in the new gemba?

Recommended Reading

Chip Heath and Dan Heath. *Made to Stick: Why Some Ideas Survive and Others Die.* Random House, New York, NY; 1st edition, January 2, 2007.

Clayton M. Christensen and Michael E. Raynor. *The Innovator's Solution: Creating and Sustaining Successful Growth.* Harvard Business School Press, Boston, MA; 1st edition, September 2003.

Edward T. Hall. *The Silent Language.* Reissue edition, New York, NY; August 1, 1973.

Edward T. Hall. *Beyond Culture.* Anchor Books, New York, NY; January 7, 1977.

Geert Hoftsede, Gert J. Hofstede, and Michael Minkov. *Cultures and Organizations: Software of the Mind.* McGraw-Hill Education, New York, 3rd edition, May 24, 2010.

Gemba Kaizen. *A Commonsense, Low-Cost Approach to Management.* Masaaki Imai. McGraw-Hill New York, NY, 1997.

Gemba Walks and James P. Womak. *Expanded Edition,* Lean Enterprise Institute, Inc, Cambridge, MA; 2nd edition, January 1, 2013.

Mike Rother and John Shook. *Learning to See: Value Stream Mapping to Add Value and Eliminate MUDA.* Lean Enterprise Institute, Cambridge, MA; SPi edition, June 1, 1999.

Pascal Dennis. *Getting the Right Things Done: A Leader's Guide to Planning and Execution.* Lean Enterprise Institute, Cambridge, MA; 1st edition, 2006.

Richard Lewis. *When Cultures Collide: Leading Across Cultures.* Nicholas Brealey Publishing, Boston, MA; 3rd edition, September 29, 2005.

Sam Yankelevitch and Claire Kuhl. *Lean Potion #9: Communication—The Next Lean Frontier.* Ashir Diss, LLC, Greenville, SC, 2014.

Index

For Product Safety Concerns and Information please contact our EU
representative GPSR@taylorandfrancis.com
Taylor & Francis Verlag GmbH, Kaufingerstraße 24, 80331 München, Germany

www.ingramcontent.com/pod-product-compliance
Ingram Content Group UK Ltd.
Pitfield, Milton Keynes, MK11 3LW, UK
UKHW051833180425
457613UK00022B/1236